TABS Manual

for the

Temperament and Atypical Behavior Scale

TABS Manual

for the

Temperament and Atypical Behavior Scale

Early Childhood Indicators of Developmental Dysfunction

by

John T. Neisworth, Ph.D.
The Pennsylvania State University

Stephen J. Bagnato, Ed.D., N.C.S.P.
University of Pittsburgh School of Medicine

John Salvia, D.Ed.
The Pennsylvania State University

Frances M. Hunt, Ph.D.
University of Virginia School of Medicine

PAUL H. BROOKES PUBLISHING CO.®

Baltimore • London • Sydney

·P A U L·H·
BROOKES
PUBLISHING Co.

Paul H. Brookes Publishing Co.
Post Office Box 10624
Baltimore, Maryland 21285-0624

www.brookespublishing.com

Second printing, January 2005.

The suggestions in this book are not intended as a substitute for professional consultation. The authors and publisher disclaim any liability arising directly or indirectly from the use of this book.

Typeset by Barton Matheson Willse & Worthington, Baltimore, Maryland.
Manufactured in the United States of America by
Versa Press, East Peoria, Illinois.

See page 2 as well as the end of this manual for information about the products making up the TABS system.

The case studies and examples used in the text are based on real individuals with disabilities. Identifying information has been changed to protect confidentiality; in some cases, individual stories have been combined or slightly altered to produce a stronger illustration.

Library of Congress Cataloging-in-Publication Data

TABS Manual for the Temperament and Atypical Behavior Scale : early childhood indicators of developmental dysfunction / John T. Neisworth . . . [et al.].
p. cm.
Includes bibliographical references and index.
ISBN 1-55766-422-6 (pbk.)
1. Developmentally disabled children—Psychological testing. 2. Behavioral assessment of children. I. Neisworth, John T.
RJ506.D47 1999
618.92'0075—dc21 99-11263
CIP

British Library Cataloguing in Publication data are available from the British Library.

TABS Contents

About the Authors vii

Acknowledgments ix

An Overview 1

Temperament and Self-Regulation: Research Foundations 7

Administering, Scoring, and Interpreting the TABS Screener and Assessment Tool 21

TABS Development 35

Technical Adequacy of TABS 51

Intervention: Guidelines for an Ecological Approach 63

Research-Based Specific Interventions 71

References 95

Appendix

Agencies and Organizations Contributing to the TABS Sample 99

Conversion Table 105

Index 107

TABS About the Authors

John T. Neisworth, Ph.D., Professor of Special Education, Coordinator for Early Intervention, The Pennsylvania State University, University Park, Pennsylvania

Dr. Neisworth is Professor of Special Education and Coordinator for Early Intervention at The Pennsylvania State University at University Park. He is author of 12 texts in early intervention and special education and has directed 10 personnel preparation projects. Dr. Neisworth is founding co-editor of the journal *Topics in Early Childhood Special Education* and serves on its board of editors as well as on the boards of *Journal of Early Intervention, Infants and Young Children, Child and Family Behavior Therapy,* and others. He is Academic Coordinator for the Pennsylvania Autism Institute and the Pennsylvania Department of Education course sequence in applied behavior analysis. Dr. Neisworth's present research focuses on family-centered approaches to early assessment and intervention.

Stephen J. Bagnato, Ed.D., N.C.S.P., Associate Professor of Pediatrics and Psychology, Children's Hospital of Pittsburgh, University of Pittsburgh School of Medicine, Pittsburgh, Pennsylvania

Dr. Bagnato is a developmental school psychologist and Associate Professor of Pediatrics and Psychology at the University of Pittsburgh School of Medicine. He is Director of the Early Childhood Diagnostic Services program at Children's Hospital of Pittsburgh and the Developmental Psychology Training Core of the UCLID (University, Community, Leaders, and Individuals with Disabilities) Center at the University of Pittsburgh, a Maternal and Child Health Bureau leadership training institute in neurodevelopmental disabilities. He is Director of Early Childhood Partnerships (Early CHILD), a community-based consultation, training, technical assistance, and research collaborative dedicated to early childhood service delivery, professional development, and public policy issues. Dr. Bagnato specializes in authentic curriculum-based assessment. He has more than 80 publications in early intervention, early childhood education, school psychology, developmental disabilities, and developmental neuropsychology. His latest book (with John T. Neisworth) is the third edition of the widely used resources text: *LINKing Assessment and Early Intervention: An Authentic Curriculum-Based Approach* (Paul H. Brookes Publishing Co., 1997).

John Salvia, D.Ed., Professor of Special Education, The Pennsylvania State University, University Park, Pennsylvania

Dr. Salvia is Professor of Special Education, a member of the School Psychology faculty, and former Head of the Department of Educational and School Psychology and Special Education at The Pennsylvania State University. He has been a Visiting Scholar at the University of Minnesota and the University of California (Los Angeles). He has been a Visiting Professor at the University of California (Santa Barbara), the University of Victoria (Canada), and the University of Sao Paulo (Brazil) as a Fulbright Fellow. He is or has been a member of the editorial board of the leading journals in special education and a consultant to numerous research centers and governmental agencies. He is the author or co-author of more than 40 research articles appearing in refereed journals, 2 books, numerous book chapters, an adaptive behavior scale, and about 50 other miscellaneous publications (e.g., reports to sponsors, Appellate Opinions for due process hearings, instructional materials).

Frances M. Hunt, Ph.D., Former Project Manager, Child–Parent Attachment Project, University of Virginia School of Medicine and Curry School of Education, Charlottesville, Virginia

Dr. Hunt was Project Manager for the Child–Parent Attachment Project, University of Virginia School of Medicine and Curry School of Education. She provided consultation and training in behavior management and early intervention for various agencies through her private practice as a behavioral consultant to families and professionals. Her previous positions include a postdoctoral fellowship in psychology at the Kennedy Krieger Institute and The Johns Hopkins University School of Medicine. She joined the faculty there and developed a community-based, family-centered clinic to assist local agencies in providing specialized early intervention services for children with severe behavior problems. As an adjunct faculty member at Loyola College of Maryland, she developed a master's degree program in Early Childhood Special Education. Dr. Hunt now resides in England, where she continues her consultation activities.

TABS

Acknowledgments

The literature research, field trials, norming, and manuscript preparation for the development of TABS were made possible by the efforts of many colleagues and assistants, whose help we gratefully acknowledge.

Special thanks to Lori M. Amos, Sylvia McDowell, Catherine Martinelli, and Jaye Herrick. Lori M. Amos's master's thesis at Penn State provided the major literature research for initial versions of TABS. Her scholarship and thoroughness gave us a great start on the literature. Sylvia McDowell was especially helpful in organizing the normative data and, with the assistance of Gretchen Brangenberg, in contributing much to the content of the final chapter on specific interventions. Catherine Martinelli and Jaye Herrick were extremely helpful in several aspects of our research, including data coding, reviewing protocols for completeness, and checking for parent consent as well as other compliance requirements.

We acknowledge the hard work of Davi Kathiresan and Eleana Shair, UCLID trainees at Children's Hospital and the University of Pittsburgh. They cataloged and organized data by diagnosis for statistical analysis.

To Glenda Carelas at Penn State went the arduous mission of typing, formatting, and producing a unified manuscript written by four authors; the effort required would have frustrated anyone without her skill and tolerance! We are indebted to Glenda, who works as an indispensable member of our professional team. We rely on her dedication to quality and understanding of the authors' idiosyncrasies and special needs in providing a final document.

We appreciate the creative, committed, and organized work of Helen McElheny at Children's Hospital, who designed and produced the original field-test versions of TABS, corresponded with agency field sites across 33 states, and ensured that each site received a full packet of information to conduct the normative study.

We continue to be grateful to the many parents, teachers, and other professionals who provided the database for TABS. From item development to field testing and norming, hard-working professionals and concerned parents gave us the motivation, collaboration, and actual data that resulted in the Temperament and Atypical Behavior Scale (see list of contributing sites in appendix, beginning on page 99). We sincerely hope their efforts will be rewarded as they add TABS to their tools for helping children and their families.

Finally, we are grateful that portions of the research activities of this book were aided by students, trainees, and faculty support by several federal and foundation grants:

- U.S. Department of Education, Office of Special Education and Rehabilitative Services, School-Linked Service Competition, Collaborative Health Interventions for Learners with Disabilities (Project CHILD): Collaborative Developmental Healthcare in Early Intervention Programs, Grant No. HO23D40013

- Jewish Healthcare Foundation of Pittsburgh, Project Early CHILD: A consultative model for developmental healthcare support in early intervention programs
- U.S. Department of Health and Human Services, Maternal and Child Health Bureau (MCHB), Interdisciplinary Leadership Education for Health Professionals Caring for Children with Neurodevelopmental Disabilities: University, Community, Leaders, and Individuals with Disabilities—UCLID Center at the University of Pittsburgh, Grant No. MCJ429414
- U.S. Department of Education, Office of Special Education Programs, Comprehensive Early Intervention (COMP-EI), Grant No. HO29Q20134-96

TABS Manual

for the

Temperament and Atypical Behavior Scale

1

An Overview

Children may be declared eligible for early intervention services for several reasons. The major basis for eligibility determination and program planning is significant delay in developmental milestone attainment. A second basis for concern is the presence of unusual, atypical behaviors. Significant levels of atypical behavior can result in developmental delays as well as confront parents and other caregivers with management challenges.

Until the mid- to late 1990s, children who manifested behavior or temperament problems were served by psychiatrists or psychologists who typically conducted their assessments by clinical observation and parent interview. Today behavior problems are more readily recognized, and assessment relies on numerous checklists and rating scales for determining children's self-regulation, temperament, and behavior patterns. Unfortunately, few of these tools are designed to assess infants and young children, and those devices that do target this population frequently suffer from a lack of norms and limited reliabilities and validities.

The Temperament and Atypical Behavior Scale (TABS) was developed to provide a reliable and valid, norm-referenced, individually administered measure of dysfunctional behavior appropriately used with infants and young children between the ages of 11 and 71 months. In developing TABS, we were guided by our own research as well as research and professional opinion dealing with the assessment and diagnosis of early childhood behavior disorders. Temperament generally refers to one's characteristic emotional style or disposition. Extremes of temperament are often regarded as socioemotional disorders that can impede general development. We defined atypical behavior as conduct that is sufficiently aberrant to 1) signal problematic, dysfunctional development, or 2) threaten present or future development. Behaviors may be quite unusual in their own right regardless of age (e.g., makes strange throat noises), when compared with same-age peers (e.g., doesn't have a regular sleep schedule), or in terms of frequency or intensity (e.g., flaps hands over and over, consistently upset by changes in daily schedule). Atypical behaviors are commonly associated with a variety of syndromes and behavior disorders.

As a norm-referenced scale, TABS is intended to identify children who are either developing atypically or are at risk for atypical development. In addition, when used for clinical purposes, TABS data can indicate specific areas of concern and can be the basis for planning early intervention programs for children and support programs for parents.

COMPONENTS

There are three components of TABS: the Screener, the Assessment Tool, and the **TABS Manual**.

TABS Screener The 15-item Screener was designed for rapid identification of children who should receive more thorough, close-up assessment for developmental issues related to temperament and self-regulation. The Screener can provide documentation of atypical functioning. It can also be routinely included in developmental assessment programs or more general screening programs. Of course, children referred because of concerns related to atypical behaviors (rather than only delays) should be assessed with the full TABS Assessment Tool.

TABS Assessment Tool The TABS Assessment Tool is a form containing a checklist of specific behaviors. Next to each behavior, there is a place for the respondent (usually one or both parents) to record whether the child in question exhibits the behavior and, if so, whether the parents need help with the behavior. In addition, there is space to document relevant information about the child, space to write both the total raw score (*Temperament and Regulatory Index [TRI]*) and the raw scores for each of the four subtests or factors, and space to record the percentiles and standard scores associated with the raw scores.

TABS Manual The TABS Manual contains seven chapters and an appendix. Chapter 1 provides an overview of TABS. Chapter 2 outlines a rationale and research basis for the scale and discusses the importance of and dysfunctions related to temperament and self-regulation. Chapter 3 provides instructions for using TABS as well as extended illustrations. Chapter 4 focuses on item development and standardization, and factor extraction, reliabilities, and validities are discussed in Chapter 5. The last two chapters (6 and 7) offer guidelines, examples, and research-based interventions for many of the behaviors identified with TABS. The appendix includes a list of agencies and organizations contributing to the TABS sample as well as a conversion table used in scoring the Assessment Tool.

CONTENT SUMMARY

On the TABS Assessment Tool, atypical self-regulatory behavior is assessed by 55 items in areas such as temperament, attention, attachment, social behavior, play, vocal and oral behavior, senses and movement, self-stimulation and self-injury, and neurobehavioral state. Four psychometric factors underlie the 55 items and are arranged into four subtests on the Assessment Tool. These four factors (referred to as factors or subtests interchangeably throughout this manual) define a construct of atypical temperament and self-regulation.

Factor 1: Detached For infants and young children, a *detached* style of temperament and self-regulation is exemplified by behavior that is withdrawn, aloof, self-absorbed, difficult to engage, and disconnected from everyday routines involving adults or other children. This behavior can be manifested in a variety of activities and contexts. Infants and young children with a detached style may *look through or past people, tune out, lose contact with what is going on, often just stare into space,* or *act like others are not there.* Behavior assessed by Subtest 1 is commonly associated with autism spectrum disorder (ASD).

Factor 2: Hyper-sensitive/active For infants and young children, a *hyper-sensitive/active* style of temperament and self-regulation is exemplified by behavior that is overreactive to even slight environmental stimulation, impulsive, highly active, negative, and defiant. This behavior can be manifested in a variety of activities and contexts. Infants and young children with a hyper-sensitive/active style may be *difficult to soothe when upset and crying; frequently irritable, touchy, or fussy; mostly on the go; too grabby, impulsive;* or *destructive.* Behavior assessed by Subtest 2 is commonly associated with attention-deficit/hyperactivity disorder (ADHD).

Factor 3: Underreactive For infants and young children, an *underreactive* style of behavior is truly unresponsive and requires intense environmental stimulation to elicit a response. An underreactive style is associated with limited awareness, low alertness, passivity, and lethargy—it differs from a detached style that *actively* avoids engagement. Infants and young children with an underreactive style may *show no surprise to new events; not be upset when a favorite toy is taken away; not react to sounds;* or *rarely smile, giggle, or laugh at funny things.* Behavior assessed by Subtest 3 is commonly associated with a variety of severe neurodevelopmental problems (i.e., problems presumed to have primarily a neural basis, such as problems related to brain injury and more subtle neurological impairment).

Factor 4: Dysregulated For infants and young children, a *dysregulated* style of temperament and self-regulation is exemplified by difficulty controlling or modulating neurophysiological behavior (e.g., sleeping, crying, self-comforting) and oral-motor control (e.g., jitteriness and hypersensitivity to physical contact). Infants and young children with problems in regulation may *cry too long, need help falling asleep too often, scream in their sleep,* or *be inconsolable.*

PURPOSES

TABS was developed to meet the increasing need to assess the presence of developmentally dysfunctional behavior rather than delayed or absent ap-

Table 1.1. Appropriate uses of TABS

Use	Description
Screening	To estimate the risk status and need for comprehensive assessment of temperament and self-regulation through large-group, communitywide screening programs
Focused assessment and eligibility determination	To assess the severity of problems in temperament and self-regulation using normative comparisons
Individualized program goal planning	To help parents and professionals identify intervention targets within individualized family service plans (IFSPs), individualized education programs (IEPs), or wraparound mental health behavioral support plans
Progress and program evaluation	To track and document specific changes in temperament and self-regulation associated with intervention
Research	To conduct research using temperament and self-regulation as predictors, dependent measures, or correlates

propriate behavior (e.g., developmental milestones). Many infants and preschoolers may not manifest developmental delays sufficient to qualify for early intervention services; nevertheless, they may exhibit difficulties in temperament and self-regulation that can result in serious behavior problems and that may lead to delayed development if untreated. Early identification and intervention may reduce the severity of these behaviors and may assist parents in coping with and managing disordered behavior.

TABS may be used alone or as part of a comprehensive assessment battery. Because TABS is norm-referenced, clinicians and service providers can compare the frequency of a child's dysfunctional behaviors to the frequency of such behaviors in children generally. Because TABS items are written in terms of behaviors or specific characteristics, they can be specifically targeted for intervention. And, because certain interventions can be suggested for each behavior and parents are encouraged to indicate whether they would like help in coping with specific problems, TABS is useful for designing individualized family service plans (IFSPs) as well as individualized education programs (IEPs) and wraparound mental health behavioral support plans.

TABS may also be used in a variety of research activities, such as evaluating the frequency of temperament and regulatory problems in groups of young children with a variety of developmental problems, ascertaining the joint occurrence of temperament and regulatory disorders with other developmental problems (e.g., social or language disorders), evaluating the effect of interventions with parents and children, and so forth.

As summarized in Table 1.1, TABS can be used for screening, determining eligibility for special services, planning education and treatment programs, monitoring program effectiveness, and conducting research.

ADMINISTRATION

The TABS Screener and Assessment Tool can be completed by the *parent or professional who knows a child's daily behavior well enough to respond* Yes *or* No *to each item.* Most parents will be able to complete the TABS Screener in 5 minutes or less and the TABS Assessment Tool in 15 minutes or less.

Parents are the preferred respondents for several reasons. First, in most cases, parents will have the best knowledge of their child's behavior at home.

Second, using information provided by parents can decrease assessment costs and professional time (Clark, Paulson, & Conlin, 1993). Third, public law and professional ethics require that parents participate in the assessment process.

Because parents are the preferred respondents, we developed administration procedures according to the guidelines for designing "parent-friendly" materials suggested by Diamond and Squires (1993) and Neisworth and Bagnato (1996). Parents should not be rushed to complete the TABS Screener or Assessment Tool. They can complete them during or after a home or office visit or be guided to complete them through a telephone interview, and they may be given additional explanations without violating the administration procedures of TABS. Although TABS items have been written at a third-grade reading level, some parents may have difficulty reading them, in which case items may be read to them, again without violating administration procedures. Finally, a professional familiar with the child can complete the Screener or Assessment Tool with input from the adults who live with the child.

TARGET BEHAVIORS

In developing items for the TABS Assessment Tool, we had a choice of two different approaches. On the one hand, we could derive items from an *a priori* classification system (e.g., *Diagnostic and Statistical Manual of Mental Disorders, Fourth Edition* [DSM-IV] [American Psychiatric Association, 1994]; *International Classification of Diseases, Ninth Edition* [ICD-9] [World Health Organization, 1989]), a particular theory (e.g., Piaget's theory of cognitive development), or some causative basis (e.g., developmental neurology). On the other hand, we could use a more pragmatic empirical approach (cf. Einfeld & Tonge, 1992) in which parents, service providers, and professionals identified atypical behavior. We chose the latter option.

An initial pool of almost 200 atypical, aberrant, and undesirable behaviors were culled from articles appearing in research journals in early intervention, child psychology, child development, developmental disabilities, school psychology, pediatrics, and behavior therapy. Almost 100 items came from the suggestions of clinicians who described atypical behavior associated with conditions such as autism, fragile X syndrome, fetal alcohol syndrome (FAS), and Williams syndrome. Finally, a few items were suggested by existing scales. This pool was reduced by eliminating behavior that was developmentally immature or delayed and behavior that was clearly learned, although dysfunctional. The remaining items were examined for redundancy and wording before field testing. The final selection of items was based on the performances of the children in the normative samples and is described in detail in Chapter 4.

ITEM SCORING

When completing the Screener or Assessment Tool, a *Yes* should be checked only if the behavior is a current (or recent) problem (i.e., either in and of itself or when compared with that of same-age children). As an example, *al-*

most never babbles or tries to talk would not be a problem when considering a 1-month-old but would be atypical for a 2-year-old. *No* is checked if the behavior does not apply (due to age expectations) or if it is not a problem for the child in question.

Items frequently call for the parent to make a judgment about the frequency (e.g., *jealous too often*), duration (e.g., *often cries too long*), or intensity (e.g., *has wild temper tantrums*) of specific behaviors. Clearly, responses to questions that require judgment calls will be subjective—what one considers excessive or problematic depends on the tolerance level of the parents being questioned, as well as other factors—yet we have found, as have others (Glascoe, 1991; Glascoe & MacLean, 1990), that when behavior is seriously atypical, parents' judgments correspond to the ratings made by professionals.

2

Temperament and Self-Regulation

Research Foundations

Common frameworks for conceptualizing early behavior problems are often based on developmentally inappropriate models of psychopathology that extend adult classification approaches to very young children. Early childhood teachers and parents need natural observational methods to detect the developmental significance of early behavior problems, to plan growth experiences for their children, and to track the progress that children in their care make in smoothing temperament and gaining self-control. The results of developmental research describing the nature of early self-regulatory behavior problems have not been applied successfully for young children either with or without special needs.

We have spent more than 10 years conducting research to develop an inventory useful for describing problems that young children show in their temperamental styles and self-regulatory capabilities associated with mild to severe developmental difficulties. The resulting inventory, *Temperament and Atypical Behavior Scale (TABS): Early Childhood Indicators of Developmental Dysfunction,* is based on developmental research in three major areas: 1) typical developmental patterns of early self-regulation, 2) developmental indicators of atypical self-regulatory characteristics, and 3) self-regulatory problems that are associated with diagnosed neurodevelopmental/neurobehavioral disorders.

DEFINITIONS

Terms such as *temperament* and *self-regulation* require some clarification before proceeding. Although each of the terms or constructs could be discussed at length, we offer brief descriptions of each for the immediate discussion.

Temperament refers to the overall behavioral style with which a particular child seems to be born; this style involves extremes in various qualitative dimensions of behavior such as activity level, excitability, ability to be consoled, involvement with others, and degree of self-control. Bates and Wachs discussed research that demonstrates that temperamental characteristics of self-regulatory capacities are "biologically rooted individual differences" that have a neurodevelopmental basis and can be observed over time as "early appearing and relatively stable dimensions of behavior" (1994, p. 18).

Self-regulation is a child's emerging capability to monitor and control his or her behaviors and overall behavioral style in response to social expectations. Kopp (1982) emphasized the typical developmental progression toward mature self-regulation proceeding from the early control of arousal, attention, and sensorimotor organization by infants to the more mature control of behavior in reaction to social rules in later childhood (4–8 years). In contrast, DeGangi (1991a, 1991b) presented a complementary framework for detecting and managing *atypical* patterns of temperament and self-regulation in young children with developmental disabilities by focusing on the general areas of emotion, attention, and sensory capacities.

Indicators refer to specific categories of unusual temperamental and self-regulatory behaviors that have been reported in the research literature to be "associated" with various neurodevelopmental disabilities. We must be cautious, of course, to emphasize that *associated* means related, but not necessarily causative. Such indicators, however, may be considered precursors of later disabilities. For example, early problems with a detached temperamental style involving poor eye contact, little social reciprocity, low verbal or nonverbal communication, and high self-stimulatory behaviors are associated with ASD.

Our research review for TABS has focused on the concept of *neurobehavioral markers* to distinguish those early precursory atypical behavior patterns that arguably have a neurological basis. Neurobehavioral markers refer to atypical self-regulatory behaviors that 1) are observed frequently in infants and young children with authenticated neurological insults, 2) indicate difficulties in various regulatory dimensions (e.g., sensory, attentional, social-emotional, neuromotor, and state organization), and 3) may offer early predictors of and discriminations among certain neurodevelopmental diagnoses.

In the TABS research, neurobehavioral markers can be classified or sorted into several atypical temperament and self-regulation response classes, such as detachment, state dysregulation, disinhibition, hypersensitivity, underreactivity, and various other brain–behavior dimensions (e.g., sleeping, eating, staring, seizure-like symptoms, repetitive behaviors). Problematic development of self-regulation is considered to be a common denominator and concern identified by research in neurobehavioral markers. Another example is the pattern of atypical social communication and hyperactivity observed in children diagnosed with fragile X syndrome.

Atypical development refers to significant delays, dysfunctions, or atypical child capabilities. Therefore, both the rate and the content of development may be atypical for chronological age or expected developmental stage. Moreover, unusual or extreme temperamental styles and self-regulatory behaviors are frequently associated with atypical developmental rate and content. In the most serious instances, the atypical development pattern and associated neurobehavioral characteristics (and sometimes physical attributes) lead to a formal diagnosis.

CONCEPTUAL AND RESEARCH SCHEMES FOR DISORDERS OF TEMPERAMENT AND SELF-REGULATION IN YOUNG CHILDREN

Few researchers have attempted to define patterns of typical and atypical development for temperament and self-regulation with particular application to infants and young children with developmental disabilities (Huntington & Simeonsson, 1993). The seminal work of Thomas and Chess (1977), the most well-known work in the area of temperament, focuses on the major dimensions of temperament and behavioral style of young children in responding to their environments. Later researchers in the area coupled the concepts of temperament and self-regulation (Bates & Wachs, 1994; Rothbart & Ahadi, 1994; Rothbart & Derryberry, 1981, 1982). Developmental research confirms the view that temperament encompasses the infant's innate, biologically based patterns of reacting to stimulation (reactivity) and the parallel capacity for emerging self-regulation. A "core set" of five temperamental attributes that are characteristic of typical development has emerged from research in this area and includes 1) novelty reactivity: fearfulness of and distress caused by novelty, 2) negative reactivity: general irritability and distress caused by frustration, 3) positive affectivity toward people and objects, 4) gross motor activity and expenditure of energy, and 5) attentional persistence. The researchers conclude that a young child's failure to develop a mature ability to inhibit or delay action (brain–behavior "executive attentional system") is strongly related to difficulties in self-regulation; impairments in this neurodevelopmentally rooted system are associated with various problems in thinking and behavioral organization.

TYPICAL DEVELOPMENTAL PROGRESSION FOR SELF-REGULATION

Kopp (1982) formulated and conducted developmental research on the emergence of self-regulatory capacities from infancy through the early childhood years. Her studies defined mature self-regulation as the capability to monitor and control one's own behavior in response to social rules and expectations. Early neurophysiological and sensorimotor processes involving arousal, attention, alertness, and state organization in infancy are viewed as the precursors for later regulation of social behavior. Kopp posed five phases of self-regulation in typical child development: 1) neurophysiological modulation (birth–3 months), 2) sensorimotor modulation (3–9+ months), 3) control (12–18 months), 4) self-control (24+ months), and 5) self-regulation (36+ months).

ATYPICAL SELF-REGULATION AND NEUROBEHAVIORAL ORGANIZATION

DeGangi (1991a, 1991b) formulated an integrated and useful scheme for understanding, assessing, and treating atypical self-regulatory disorders and their patterns. Her clinical research focused on the sensory, emotional, and attentional problems of "fussy" or "difficult" infants and young children who are at most serious risk of developing the maladaptive self-regulatory patterns associated with ASD, ADHD, and oppositional-defiant and conduct disorders. DeGangi proposed four levels of neurobehavioral organization and the self-regulatory dysfunctions that occur when development is impaired at each level or stage: 1) regulatory disorders of basic sensory/neurophysiological organization, 2) regulatory disorders of dynamic coordination of neurophysiological and sensory homeostasis, 3) regulatory disorders of overt behaviors in noncontingent social situations, and 4) regulatory disorders of overt behavior in contingent social situations.

A neurodevelopmental research consortium (Lester, Tronick, & Mayes, 1993) conducted research on the neurobehavioral and neurophysiological effects of prenatal cocaine exposure in infants. Their studies posited that cocaine might affect neurobehavioral regulation in "the four A's of infancy"—the processes of arousal, attention, affect, and action. In this respect, problems in these areas may be seen as neurobehavioral markers that signal dysfunctions in the development of temperament and self-regulation in young children.

DIAGNOSTIC CLASSIFICATION OF REGULATORY DISORDERS

The Diagnostic Classification: 0–3 (DC:0–3) (ZERO TO THREE: National Center for Infants, Toddlers, and Families, 1994) is a unique and developmentally appropriate framework for conceptualizing and classifying mental health and developmental disorders in infancy and early childhood. DC:0–3 is innovative as an early childhood disorders diagnostic scheme in that it posits a transactional model rather than a psychopathological model to describe behavior differences in early development. DC:0–3 highlights the relationships among the infant's temperament, neurophysiological differences, and self-regulatory behavior. Diagnosis is not viewed as immutable but rather as modified in response to interventions that involve the child, the family, and the environment.

> Through systematic observation . . . a more sophisticated understanding has emerged of the factors that contribute to adaptive and maladaptive patterns of development and the meaning of individual differences in infancy. . . .Timely assessment and accurate diagnosis can provide the foundation for effective interventions before early deviations become consolidated into maladaptive patterns of functioning. (1994, p. 3)

Regulatory disorder in DC:0–3 is one of the central descriptive classifications for self-regulatory difficulties and temperamental extremes that, if untreated, may later be consolidated as serious developmental and mental health disorders (e.g., ADHD, ASD, pervasive developmental disorder [PDD]). Regulatory disorders are characterized by infants and preschoolers having great difficulty "regulating behavior and physiological, sensory, attentional, motor or affective processes, and in organizing a calm, alert, or affectively positive state" (p. 31). The DC:0–3 manual identifies four types of conceptually based and clinically derived regulatory disorders, which TABS research has validated empirically: 1) *Hypersensitive;* 2) *Underreactive;*

3) *Motorically Disorganized, Impulsive;* and 4) *Other or Motor-Sensory Processing Difficulty.*

EXTREMES IN TEMPERAMENTAL STYLES

Early childhood researchers view wide individual differences in the behavior characteristics associated with various temperaments as extremes that influence the quality of parent–child and child–environment interactions (Chess & Thomas, 1986). Two major styles of temperament are posited in which extremes are observed: difficult and slow-to-warm. These styles are discussed in more detail in the next paragraph. Extremes in temperament are often seen in specific behavioral dimensions, including activity level, regularity of behavior and mood or rhythmicity, approach–withdrawal, adaptability, threshold of responsiveness, intensity of reaction, quality of mood, distractibility, attention span, and persistence. Early intervention professionals may become aware of concerns about behavior influenced by temperamental characteristics in four instances: 1) extremes in one or more temperamental traits that are within the wide typical range may appear deviant to parents or teachers and may create problems for the child's capacity to adapt to and master his or her environment; 2) a particular temperamental characteristic may become exaggerated and maladaptive when the child has repeated unsuccessful interactions with people and situations; 3) a generalized behavior disorder can result when the child's overall interactions with the environment are unusually negative and unsuccessful; and 4) as a result of a physical impairment, neurodevelopmental disorder, or affective and communicative disorder, the child may exhibit temperamental characteristics that are exaggerated and that compound the impact of the disability on the child's interactions with his or her environment.

In typical extremes of temperament, children with "difficult" styles of behavior (10%–15% of children in national longitudinal samples) have the most difficulty with self-regulation. This style is usually characterized by irregularity in reactions to the environment and in establishing sleeping and feeding routines, irritability and fussiness, intense levels of reactivity, slow or poor adaptation to and coping with new social situations, and low persistence. Perhaps the most ubiquitous example is the difficult, highly active child who is viewed by teachers and parents as having ADHD. The "slow-to-warm" child can show extremes in shyness (which may be misjudged as ASD), anxiousness, timidity, and fearfulness. A child with low activity may be viewed as depressed, sluggish, and even delayed in development.

Children who show exaggerations in one or more temperamental characteristics often have difficulty adjusting to the modal expectations for children of a certain age, particularly in preschool classrooms. Too much pressure or demand to conform or adapt quickly to new or group situations often creates stress for the child and leads to extreme reactions. For example, the persistent child who "needs" to finish a task beyond the time limit may throw a tantrum or show anxiety when removed prematurely. The failure of caregivers to adjust demands to the infant or young child's individual temperament often reinforces negative behavior and creates repeated occasions in which the child fails and is disapproved of by adults. In extreme instances, the mismatch between the child's temperamental style and the responses of caregivers at home and preschool creates a permanently maladaptive pattern of behavior that is consistent across situations and people; this pattern then meets the definition for a behavior disorder.

Children with established neurodevelopmental disabilities and related syndromes often present exaggerated examples of the mismatch between temperamental style and the functional effect of the child's impairment on everyday adaptation and self-regulation involving social skills, forethought, social communication, and motor control. Young children with severe neuromotor impairments often learn to be helpless and become sad, lethargic, and sometimes stressed because of the failure of their behavior to effectively operate on their environments (prosthetic devices and augmentative and alternative communication systems work to ease the debilitating effect of their disabilities). Young children with seizure disorders and neuromotor problems have great difficulty because they are often hypersensitive to sights, sounds, and changes in position; this temperamental characteristic is exaggerated in highly stimulating environments and leads to tantrums and other extreme reactions of social withdrawal. Teachers and caregivers must be sensitive to the interactions among a child's functional impairments, individual temperament, and the complexity of environmental stimulation in order to adjust the situation accordingly to allow the child to function optimally.

NEUROBEHAVIORAL MARKERS OF EARLY REGULATORY DISORDERS ASSOCIATED WITH NEURODEVELOPMENTAL DISABILITIES

Emerging research documents the recurring patterns or clusters of behavioral symptoms (markers) that distinguish certain neurological and genetic syndromes and neurodevelopmental disabilities. Despite the overlap of symptoms among syndromes, researchers may be able to generate "atypical self-regulatory templates" to help practitioners discriminate among disorders and to signal the need for both early interventions and medical follow-up. Developmental medicine refers to these markers as *neurobehavioral phenotypes,* suggestive of a neurological or genetic basis. Some examples of difficulties that these phenotypes, or neurobehavioral markers of atypical self-regulation, can help identify include fragile X syndrome, ASD, and ADHD. The following sections review some of the major neurodevelopmental and neurobehavioral disorders and their reported associated neurobehavioral markers of atypical self-regulation. It should be cautioned, however, that much more focused empirical research is needed to confirm neurobehavioral phenotypes for specific disorders, especially in infancy and early childhood.

Regulatory Disorders

With the publication of DC:0–3, the observations of many interventionists in interdisciplinary fields that emphasize the unique qualities of infants and young children with special needs were codified. One of the most prominent contributions of DC:0–3 was the diagnosis of regulatory disorders. As described previously in the work of DeGangi (1991a, 1991b), Emde, Katz, and Thorpe (1978), and Greenspan (1991), among others, a *regulatory disor-*

der refers to the multisystem difficulties of young children who show various problems in temperamental style and self-regulation. In effect, many young children are better described as having transient or continuous problems in self-regulation because of difficulties involving extremes in attention, emotional behavior, sensory sensitivities, state modulation, and other neurophysiological processes (e.g., sleeping; eating; coordinating sucking, swallowing, and breathing; staring). Intervention is then targeted at teaching children to modulate their own symptoms and to build self-regulatory skills in order to prevent or ameliorate maladaptive behavior patterns before they become intractable as more serious and identifiable developmental psychopathologies such as ASD and ADHD.

Fragile X Syndrome

Fragile X syndrome is the most common inherited cause of mental retardation or learning problems in both males and females (Dykens, Hodapp, & Leckman, 1994). It is an X-linked disorder carried by the mother. Children with fragile X syndrome have common variations in physical features, behavior, and developmental functioning. Common physical features include long, wide, or protruding ears; long face; flattened nasal bridge; and high arched palate. Mental retardation, learning disabilities, and even ASD are associated with fragile X syndrome (Dykens et al., 1994).

The most frequently observed and reported neurobehavioral markers for fragile X syndrome in males include social problems with peers, atypical quality of communication, unusual reactions to sensory stimulation, repetitive behaviors, and hyperactivity. For females, depressed affect, hyperactivity, and socially withdrawn behaviors are most prevalent. Studies with infants and young children are only now beginning and are much needed. Numerous studies are ongoing in major university-associated hospital centers (e.g., The Johns Hopkins University, University of North Carolina at Chapel Hill) to extend our current limited knowledge of fragile X syndrome in early and later years (Baumgardner, Reiss, Freund, & Abrams, 1995; Freund, 1994).

Autism Spectrum Disorder

ASD is considered to have a neurobiological etiology as well as evidence of a hereditary transmission. Much controversy exists regarding the relationship between fragile X syndrome and ASD because an overlap of symptoms is evident, although some researchers emphasize the differences in quality and severity as the distinguishing factors. ASD is a neurobiological disorder characterized by a triad of core "detached" behavioral features that vary in quality and prominence leading to a spectrum of mild to severe expression of the disorder. The three features involve impaired social skills and social relatedness; impaired language and social communication capabilities; and restricted interests, including stereotyped behaviors and self-stimulatory patterns. Siegel (1994, 1996) is perhaps the most prominent researcher focusing on infants and young children with ASD. Her dedication to early detection of ASD has demonstrated the developmentally inappropriate quality of traditional psychiatric frameworks for psychopathology applied to young children with suspected or confirmed ASD. Her developmental research formulated a modified DSM-IV framework, which includes imitation and pretend play and which underscores several early landmark behavioral processes for screening and assessing ASD.

Attention-Deficit/Hyperactivity Disorder

Comparatively little research has been conducted on preschoolers with hyperactive and disruptive behaviors, and considerably less with toddlers (Blackman, Westervelt, Stevenson, & Welch, 1991; Campbell, 1990; McIntosh & Cole-Love, 1996; Thomas & Tidmarsh, 1997). Preschool children in the toddler to late preschool period are frequently referred to mental health clinics or early intervention programs because of extreme behaviors relating to inattention, overactivity, temper tantrums, and aggression; nevertheless, young children who display this unregulated behavioral style represent a mixed group with many risk factors and/or potential causes, including constitutional temperamental pattern, divorce, abuse and neglect, parent–child relationship breakdowns, and other health and social conditions. Because of the undifferentiated nature of development during the early childhood years, it is difficult, if not inappropriate, to clearly define attention-deficit and hyperactivity as a disorder during this period. The results of the limited research in this area consistently couple a variety of response classes to suggest this early diagnosis, including poor selective and sustained attention, overactivity, impulsiveness, extreme temper tantrums, aggressive behavior, defiant outbursts, and irritability; nevertheless, in a study of 35 preschoolers, parents' and teachers' observations and ratings were congruent on the core characteristics of children independently diagnosed with ADHD: high activity level, high distractibility, and low persistence (McIntosh & Cole-Love, 1996). Parents and teachers, however, each reported a distinguishing temperamental profile for the ADHD group when other dimensions were graphed, perhaps reflecting different situational demands placed on the children, with parents citing high activity level, poor adaptability, high emotional intensity, low ease of management, and low persistence and teachers citing high activity level, high emotional intensity, high distractibility, and low persistence.

Fetal Alcohol Syndrome and Drug Exposure

Numerous studies have focused on the presumed effects, both transient and enduring, of fetal alcohol and drug exposure (especially cocaine) on infants and preschoolers. FAS, fetal alcohol effects (FAE), and fetal drug exposure are reported to manifest similar neurobehavioral effects reflecting central nervous system (CNS) insult (Streissguth, 1997), even though controversy exists regarding the pervasive and continuous impact of those early effects. Lester and colleagues (1991) focused the neurobehavioral effect of early cocaine exposure on four areas: arousal, attention, affect, and action. Specific neurobehavioral symptoms involve two syndromes, excitable and depressed, as observed in crying patterns with, respectively, longer duration and higher frequencies and longer latencies and fewer utterances. Meta-reviews of other research (Chapman, Worthington, Cook, & Mayfield, 1992) focus on the potential developmental and educational effects of early cocaine exposure with particular stress on high activity levels, possible seizures or disconnectedness, inattention, failure to achieve a calm state necessary to facilitate positive social interactions, and general dysregulation.

FAS and FAE have both neurophysiological and related neurodevelopmental sequelae (Burgess & Streissguth, 1990; Phelps & Grabowski, 1992; Streissguth, Herman, & Smith, 1978). Neurophysiological features involve growth impairment, short palpebral fissures (eye slits), long smooth philtrum (area between nose and lips), thin upper lip, flat midfacial area, and CNS dysfunction. Specific neurobehavioral effects that are clearly associated with CNS insults in infants and preschool children with FAS or its effects involve the following traits: neuromotor dysregulation and impairments; weak sucking response with poor feeding; tremulousness; fitful sleeping; irritability; hyperexcitability; hyperactivity (for 85% of children with FAS); mild to severe attention deficits; lack of stranger anxiety; clingy behavior with little sense of social boundaries in interaction with others; impulsivity; difficulty with situational transitions; restlessness; poor tolerance of frustration; general difficulty developing mature self-control behaviors; hypersensitivity to lights and sounds; poor social judgment; and being the target of teasing and bullying behavior.

Seizure Disorder

Classification of epilepsy or seizure disorder is divided into two categories: partial seizures, those that begin in a portion of one particular hemisphere, and generalized seizures, those that begin in a widespread fashion in both hemispheres (Brunquell, 1994). Individuals do not have to lose consciousness to experience a seizure—sudden behavioral changes may be one signal of a partial type of seizure. The involvement of various areas of the brain in an "epilepsy syndrome" may lead to different neurobehavioral sequelae. Children with early onset intractable seizures are reported to show difficulties in combining skills for successful social interaction (including focusing attention; reciprocity; nonverbal communication involving eye gaze, smiling, and other facial cues; and reaching and pointing to initiate and sustain communication) and in improvement after brain surgery (Caplan et al., 1992). Aman, Werry, and Turbott (1992) studied the behavior of young children with both partial and generalized seizure disorders. Children with partial seizures were observed and rated to be more aggressive and to have more difficulty with social interactions than children with generalized seizures. Teachers emphasized the problems with hyperactivity and overall self-regulation of aggressive behavior in children with seizures compared with a matched normative sample. Parents stressed problems in several areas including following rules; attention; overactivity; and aggressive, odd, anxious, and socially withdrawn behaviors.

Neurofibromatosis

Neurofibromatosis (NF) is one of the most prevalent gene disorders (1 in every 4,000 live births) that has wide neurobehavioral and neurodevelopmental effects (Dilts et al., 1996). NF is an autosomal dominant condition that results in a gene mutation (NF-1) and abnormal cell growth and differentiation of various tissues, especially in the central and peripheral nervous systems. Studies have focused on the prevalence of learning disabilities in NF but have shown little more specificity in profiling the typical behavioral phenotype. Regarding neurobehavioral sequelae particularly, parents and teachers report concerns about various internalized versus externalized behavior problems: anxious and sad behaviors, underreactivity, acting young for age, clumsiness, being frequently teased by others, poor social interactions, and few friendships.

Williams Syndrome

Williams syndrome (WS) is a genetic disorder of unknown etiology with specific physical and neurobehavioral features. Physical features include prenatal growth impairment, prominent lips, midfacial differences, hoarse voice, cardiovascular system anomalies, and mental retardation. Tome, Williamson, and Pauli (1990) reported that children with WS are described anecdotally as talkative, affectionate, charming, open, and gentle; however, few studies have detailed the neurobehavioral phenotype. Their research focused on the distinguishing temperamental profile of WS using the Carey temperament scales for 564 children and families between ages 12 months and 12 years. Their results showed that infants with WS compared with typical infants have greater social approach skills and lower persistence, fretfulness, and feeding problems. In children with WS who are 36 months of age and older, significant differences are observed in higher activity, lower rhythmicity, greater social approach, lower adaptability, greater intensity of reaction to stimuli, more negative mood, lower persistence, greater distractibility, and lower thresholds for negative stimulation. Overall, 66% of the children with WS were classified on the Carey temperament scale in the difficult or intermediate-high temperament clusters.

Rett Syndrome

Van Acker (1991) presented the full profile and neurobehavioral characteristics of the serious, degenerative condition known as Rett syndrome (RS). RS is a phenotypically distinct and progressive neurological disorder with a specific pattern of cognitive, functional, and physical degenerative aspects that most often affects females. Children with RS follow a characteristic developmental course. The criteria for diagnosis involve apparently typical prenatal and perinatal development for the first 6 months (especially motor skills), typical head size at birth with decelerations in head growth between 5 months and 4 years, loss of acquired purposeful hand movements, stereotypic hand movements, and motor declines with ataxic movements in walking gait. From 6 to 18 months, children show a slowing of motor development with congenital hypotonia (low muscle tone), dyskinetic disturbance of hand movements (repetitive hand wringing), twisting of arms and wrists, circulating hand–mouth movements, and involuntary opening and closing of fingers as well as excess levels of hand patting. From 1 to 3 years of age, children with RS show a loss of previously acquired abilities in social interaction, cognitive skills in play, and purposeful hand use and speech. Parents report specific neurobehavioral aspects, such as irritability, spontaneous tantrums, stereotyped movements that are continuous during wakefulness, and seizure activity and/or frequent staring spells. From 2 to 10 years of age, children with RS display some reduction in detached behaviors with increases in social interaction; however, their severe degree of mental retardation becomes pronounced and is accompanied by jerky movements and motor spasticity or rigidity or both.

Sotos Syndrome

Rutter and Cole (1991) explained that Sotos syndrome, or cerebral gigantism, is a relatively rare genetic disorder that is found mostly in females and has well-defined physical features as criteria, although the psychological or developmental and behavioral characteristics have been less well documented. Children with Sotos syndrome are large for their gestational age and have accelerated growth patterns, especially notable during infancy. Other associated physical features (not present in all cases) include high forehead, prominent protrusion of the forehead, prominent jaw, wide-spaced eyes, and a high arched palate in the mouth. These children also exhibit mental retardation and learning disabilities, especially reading difficulties. Parent and teacher ratings of behavior problems include general concerns about unusual behaviors, anxiousness, hyperactivity, precocious sexual behavior, sleep problems, problems settling into routines, excessive eating and drinking, fears, some ritualistic repetitive behaviors, little awareness of danger, poor peer social interactions, solitary play preferences, and some evidence of staring and seizures in a small subsample.

Acquired Brain Injury

Acquired brain injury in infants and young children is most often the result of trauma, both nonaccidental, such as child abuse, and accidental, such as falls and motor vehicle and tricycle/bicycle accidents. Major head trauma with coma lasting more that 24 hours frequently results in enduring neurological, neurodevelopmental, and neurobehavioral impairments. Even individual instances of "minor" acquired brain injury with no associated loss of consciousness have been implicated in subtle neurodevelopmental and neurobehavioral difficulties (Bagnato & Feldman, 1989).

The assessment of status and recovery from acquired brain injury involves measures of both development and behavior. Sensitive indicators of the presence of brain insults with respect to temperament and self-regulation include motor incoordination, hypersensitivities, staring, capacity for selective and sustained attention, delays in responding, word-finding difficulties, motor-planning difficulties, disorganized play routines, easy frustration, and variable alertness and awareness.

TABS NORMATIVE RESEARCH AS EMPIRICAL VALIDATION OF THE REGULATORY DISORDERS AXIS OF THE DIAGNOSTIC CLASSIFICATION SYSTEM

DC:0–3 (ZERO TO THREE, 1994) is a landmark development in the design of a diagnostic framework for infant and early childhood behavior that is developmentally appropriate, intervention based, and compatible with recommended practices in the early intervention field (Bagnato, 1998).

It should be noted that the DC:0–3 classifications are based on expert consensus (i.e., a pooling and agreement among professionals based on clinical opinion and logic). To paraphrase this manual's introduction, task force members believed that creation of a diagnostic classification system should proceed by pooling clinical cases for discussion by experts. Through consensus of clinical and research experts, preliminary conceptualizations were formulated. Additional data were collected and analyzed, leading to changes and refinements in the initial system. This process is ongoing in order to provide an expanding information base for further refinement of the diagnostic system. TABS, however, is based on empirical, prospective research and both benefits from and adds confirmation to the DC:0–3 efforts.

> In any scientific enterprise, but particularly in a new field, a healthy tension exists between the desire to analyze findings from systematic research before offering even initial conceptualizations, and the need to disseminate preliminary conceptualizations so that they can serve as a basis for collecting systematic data, which can lead to more empirically based efforts. The history of such efforts reflects the need for a balanced interaction between these two positions. The development of DC:0–3 represents an important first step: the presentation of expert consensus-based categorizations of mental health and developmental disorders in the early years of life. (ZERO TO THREE, 1994, p. 11)

In a previous research article on the first phase of our normative research on TABS (previously TRIAD and NIAD), Neisworth, Bagnato, and Salvia (1995) presented empirical data on nearly 300 infants and preschoolers that favorably compared and aligned the factor structure of the scale with the four conceptual/theoretical types of regulatory disorders posed and described in DC:0–3. Our current published normative data on more than 800 infants, toddlers, and preschoolers (11–71 months) further confirm our previous work and validate the four regulatory disorder types in DC:0–3 through the four statistical factors in TABS.

Regulatory disorders in the DC:0–3 diagnostic system are defined as "first evident in infancy and early childhood . . . [and] characterized by the infant or young child's difficulties in regulating behavior and physiological, sensory, attentional, motor or affective processes, and in organizing a calm, alert, or affectively positive state" (ZERO TO THREE, 1994, p. 31). Diagnosis of a regulatory disorder involves both a distinguishing pattern of behavior and evidence of difficulties with sensorimotor or organizational processing or both.

Four types of regulatory disorders are posited in the DC:0–3 system: Type I: *Hypersensitive*; Type II: *Underreactive*; Type III: *Motorically Disorganized, Impulsive*; and Type IV: *Other or Motor-Sensory Processing Difficulty* (exhibiting a motor or sensory processing difficulty but no distinct behavior pattern). The *Hypersensitive* type is assumed to consist of two patterns of behavior: one fearful and cautious and the other negative and defiant. Motor and sensory processing patterns are characterized by such indicators as overreactivity to touch, noises, lights, movement, and motor-planning difficulties. *Underreactive* regulatory disorders are reported to be identified by patterns of withdrawn, difficult-to-engage, and self-absorbed behaviors. Motor and sensory processing involves underreactivity to sights, sounds, movements, and touch and variable capacity to focus and engage with others in imaginative play or isolated play. The *Motorically Disorganized, Impulsive* type seems to be distinguished by poor self-control, a craving for sensory stimulation, and behaviors such as aggressiveness, fearlessness, impulsivity, and general disorganization in both motor and sensory domains. Finally, the *Other or Motor-Sensory Processing Difficulty* type shows neurophysiological indicators of self-regulatory distress but no clearly identifiable behavior pattern.

Table 2.1 compares the four TABS empirical factors with the four DC:0–3 regulatory disorder conceptual types. Note that the TABS *Hyper-sensitive/active* factor 2 is one of the two strongest statistical factors and stands alone to validate the DC:0–3 *Hypersensitive* Type I. However, it also encompasses the DC:0–3 *Motorically Disorganized, Impulsive* Type III; creating a superfactor that seems to involve both high reactivity in terms of low stimulation thresholds as well as active stimulus craving and negative-defiant behavior. The TABS *Detached* factor 1 and the TABS *Underreactive* factor 3 subdivide the DC:0–3 *Underreactive* Type II and validate it while also providing greater diagnostic detail for the withdrawn/difficult-to-engage and self-absorbed aspects; moreover, the TABS *Underreactive* factor 3 compared with the TABS *Detached* factor 1 distinguishes between self-regulatory disorders that are characterized by active disengagement as opposed to passive disengagement, suggesting a neurobehavioral dimension with the *Underreactive* style that may be neurophysiological in origin and a brain–behavior impairment for such children. Finally, the TABS *Dysregulated* factor 4, although statistically weak, seems to offer greater substance to the DC:0–3 *Other or Motor-Sensory Processing Difficulty* Type IV. This *Dysregulated* factor indicates neurophysiological difficulties in organization and self-regulation, mostly for state-control variables such as sleeping, eating, and modulation of emotions.

CONCLUSION

Developmental research has established the foundation for using the concepts of temperament and self-regulation for early detection and management of early behavior problems. Extremes in temperamental style show

Table 2.1. Comparison of TABS empirical factors and DC:0–3 regulatory disorder conceptual types

TABS Factor	DC:0–3 Type
1. Detached 3. Underreactive	II. Underreactive
2. Hyper-sensitive/active	I. Hypersensitive III. Motorically Disorganized, Impulsive
4. Dysregulated	IV. Other or Motor-Sensory Processing Difficulty

the types of behavioral dimensions that affect the capacity of young children to adapt and thrive in new situations. The developmental progressions of both typical and atypical self-regulation set the stage for designing early screening and assessment systems. Moreover, with ongoing research, it may be possible to identify neurobehavioral phenotypes that distinguish one class of atypical neurodevelopmental disorders or syndromes from another, thereby paving the way for more targted early intervention services.

3

Administering, Scoring, and Interpreting the TABS Screener and Assessment Tool

This chapter explains how to administer, score, and interpret the TABS Screener and Assessment Tool. The chapter ends with a demonstration of how to link interventions from the final two chapters of this manual with child behavior.

DIRECTIONS FOR ADMINISTERING THE TABS SCREENER AND ASSESSMENT TOOL

Cautions

First, professionals who use these materials should explain the nature of the task and the items to parents, surrogates, or other professionals who will be completing the items. They should be told that they will be completing a scale that contains 15 items (if using the Screener) or 55 items (if using the Assessment Tool). For each item, they are to check *Yes* or *No*. On the Assessment Tool, they are to check the *Need Help* box for those items for which there may be special concern and when assistance is wanted to cope with the behavior or situation.

Next, it is a good idea to forewarn the rater about the negative nature of the items. Parents and caregivers may become defensive or even deny their children's undesirable behavior or characteristics. We have found it helpful to tell raters (and especially parents) that all scales are designed to find what a child does and does not do. Some scales ask about a child's successes, but this scale asks about areas in which there are difficulties. Parents can also be told that almost all behavior is on a continuum, and the difference between a problem and the lack of a problem is a matter of degree.

Many children may exhibit some of these problems some of the time, and children with typical development may demonstrate many of these behaviors, although at a different intensity or duration. It is very important to tell parents that perhaps only a few items will apply to their child, but they need to answer each item carefully and accurately. Emphasize that they should consider each item before checking a box.

Finally, explain to the parent or professional the criteria for answering *Yes* and *No.* The rater should mark the box (using a check, an *X*, a slash, or whatever) in the *No* column if the behavior or characteristic is not a problem. Also, items should be marked *No* if they are not applicable because of age considerations; for example, *almost always refuses to do what is told* would not apply to a 12-month-old. The rater should mark the box in the *Yes* column only if the problematic behavior or characteristic is currently a problem.

Completing Background Information

It is critical that TABS Screener users make sure they have complete identifying data to permit follow-up with the full Assessment Tool if warranted. Whenever possible, complete Section I on the TABS Screener and Assessment Tool before the rater completes the instrument.

Completing the TABS Screener and Assessment Tool

Typically, the TABS Screener and Assessment Tool should be completed in the presence of a professional; although the forms were designed to be quickly and easily completed independently by most parents, sometimes raters will need assistance. (Completion with and without assistance was included in TABS standardization.) The general rule is that raters may be given whatever assistance they need to understand an item. An item may be read to the parent, translated into another language, or explained. Of course, no help should be given in deciding if an item represents or does not represent a problem. For example, if a parent asks, "Shawn does *X*; is that a problem?" The professional should reflect the question and scoring criteria back to the parent by saying, "If it is a problem for you, check *Yes*; if not, check *No.*" Tell the parents to mark the *Need Help* box whenever they have a special concern or want assistance for that problem. Usually, the TABS Screener is completed in about 5 minutes, and the TABS Assessment Tool is completed in less than 15 minutes.

SCORING AND INTERPRETING THE TABS SCREENER AND ASSESSMENT TOOL

Computing the TABS Screener Raw Score

For the Screener, count the number of items that were checked *Yes,* and write that number in the box labeled *Raw Score* at the bottom of the page. Although the TABS Screener was designed to reflect the four factors underlying the TABS Assessment Tool, the Screener total score should only be used to *estimate* the *Temperament and Regulatory Index (TRI),* which will be calculated on the Assessment Tool. The professional should never attempt to infer subtest performance from the Screener.

Interpreting the TABS Screener Raw Score

If the sum is 1 or 2, the child is likely to be at risk, and if the sum is 3 or more, atypical development of temperament and self-regulation is likely. (The calculations used to determine cutoff scores are discussed in more depth at the end of Chapter 4.) To be certain that a child with regulatory problems is not overlooked, we recommend that the entire TABS Assessment Tool be completed for any child with a score of 1 or more on the Screener. (Figure 3.6 shows completed items on the TABS Screener.)

Completing the TABS Assessment Tool Summary

Count the number of items in the *Detached* subtest that were checked *Yes,* and write that number in the box at the end of the subtest. Do the same for the *Hyper-sensitive/active, Underreactive,* and *Dysregulated* subtests. Transfer these four counts to the Raw Scores column on the last page of the TABS Assessment Tool. Add the four raw scores and write this total next to *Temperament & Regulatory Index (TRI).* Finally, determine percentiles and standard scores (or T-scores) of each of these raw scores by using the conversion table found in the appendix of this manual, and place those figures in the spaces provided. (For example, a *TRI* raw score of 10 corresponds to a percentile of 6, and a *Detached* raw score of 1 corresponds to a T-score of 47.)

Interpreting the Temperament and Regulatory Index *(TRI)* of the TABS Assessment Tool

In most instances, only the percentile or the standard score for a child's *TRI* (i.e., total raw score) should be reported and interpreted because the *TRI* is sufficiently reliable and stable to be used in making a variety of important decisions. Percentiles are usually understood by parents and professionals. (For example, a child who earns a percentile of 70 has a raw score equal to or better than raw scores of 70% of the children in the normative sample.) For those professionals who prefer to use standard scores, the *TRI* has two types, both with means (*M*) of 100 and standard deviations (*SD*) of 15. The standard scores (*SS*) are based on the actual (nontypical) distribution of *TRI* scores. The normalized standard scores (*SSnd*) have been transformed so that the standard scores and percentiles have the same relationship they would have if the distribution were typical. Figure 3.1 shows a TABS Assessment Tool Results section with the *TRI* completed.

In many cases, TABS will be used to identify children who are at risk for or clearly manifest atypical temperament and self-regulation. Rather than select some arbitrary cutoff score for this classification, we compared *TRI* raw score distributions for children known to have atypical development with those presumed to have typical development. As illustrated in Figures 4.2 through 4.6, the raw score distributions of children with and without disabilities for each TABS score cross at some point. For the *TRI* distribution (Figure 4.2), the raw score associated with the point where the distributions cross (i.e., 5) is equally likely to be earned by children with and without disabilities; lower raw scores (i.e., 0 to 4) are more likely to be earned by children without disabilities, while higher raw scores (i.e., 6 or more) are more likely to be earned by children with disabilities. *TRI* scores

	Raw Scores	Percentile	Standard Score (or T-score)
Detached	4		
Hyper-sensitive/active	5		
Underreactive	1		
Dysregulated	2		
Temperament & Regulatory Index (TRI) (total of four factor raw scores)	12	3	60

Figure 3.1. A TABS Assessment Tool without derived scores for subtests.

from 5 to 9 indicate a child is *at risk* for atypical temperament and/or self-regulation because those scores are earned equally or more often by children with disabilities. A raw score of 10 or more is earned by only 6.9% of children developing typically, while 60.4% of children with identified atypical development receive such scores. Because scores of 10 or more are relatively unusual, we believe *children receiving a score of 10 or more* are appropriately classified as having atypical development (i.e., serious difficulties in temperament and/or self-regulation).

Interpreting Subtest Scores of the TABS Assessment Tool

In many research and clinical environments, professionals will be interested in a child's score on one or more of the four TABS subtests. The conversion table in the appendix of this manual provides percentiles, T-scores and normalized T-scores (M = 50; SD = 10); however, we caution clinicians that subtest scores (as well as differences between subtests) are less reliable than the full *TRI.* Chapter 4 provides information that may be useful in interpreting subtest performance, such as the overlap of distributions of children with and without atypical development, and Chapter 5 provides information about subtest standard errors of measurement (*SEM*) and the reliability of differences between subtests. Figure 3.2 shows the same TABS Assessment Tool Results section as seen in Figure 3.1 with percentiles and T-scores for the subtests as well as the *TRI.*

	Raw Scores	Percentile	Standard Score (or T-score)
Detached	4	3	23
Hyper-sensitive/active	5	9	34
Underreactive	1	15	42
Dysregulated	2	5	29
Temperament & Regulatory Index (TRI) (total of four factor raw scores)	12	3	60

Figure 3.2. A TABS Assessment Tool with derived scores for subtests.

Interpreting *Need Help* Indicators

The professional should discuss each *Need Help* indicator with the parents to ascertain the nature of help wanted—more information, further assessment, consultation, direct intervention, and so forth. We recommend asking parents to prioritize their requests. (It may be possible that several problems may be addressed through a single intervention effort—see Chapter 6.) Of course, the areas in which parents indicate that they need help can provide goals for intervention plans (e.g., IFSPs, IEPs, wraparound mental health behavioral support plans).

SCORE CUTOFFS FOR PROGRAM ELIGIBILITY AND WRAPAROUND MENTAL HEALTH BEHAVIORAL SUPPORT

It is common for early intervention programs to be directed by different lead agencies for birth to 3 years (e.g., departments of child development, child and maternal health, and mental health) and for 3–5 years (departments of education). Often, different service eligibility criteria are used depending on the lead agency and its mandate. Typically, birth-to-3 programs use more flexible criteria based on some combination of quantitative cutoff scores and qualitative clinical judgment about the existing risk status of the child (e.g., low birth weight, prematurity, family need, genetic syndrome). Programs serving 3- to 5-year-old children often base their service criteria on quantitative cutoff scores only. Typical quantitative criteria for early intervention service eligibility are –1.5 standard deviations in one or two of six developmental domains or 25% delay in chronological age in those domains. Behavior problems (in the absence of delays) are often not regarded as a sufficient basis for eligibility. Early intervention providers regularly report that they need normative materials to allow them to document program eligibility in the social-emotional and behavioral domains. TABS provides parents and professionals with norm-referenced quantitative data on the frequency or extent of atypical behavior to provide an evaluation independent of clinical judgments.

TABS scores are useful in meeting criteria for early intervention program eligibility and for wraparound mental health behavioral support. The –1.5 *SD* cutoff for the *TRI* is 8, which translates to a percentile of 11 and a standard score of 78. (Recall that the TABS *TRI* is based on an average of 100 with a standard deviation of 15.) For parents, this index indicates that their child has greater self-regulatory behavior difficulties than 89% (almost 9 out of 10) of other same-age children. In all states, recommendations for wraparound mental health behavioral support (including positive behavioral support) funded by Medicaid and other programs must be accompanied by a mental health diagnosis. We believe these wraparound standards should be based on TABS normative cutoffs; our normative data suggest that a *TRI* of 5 (i.e., a percentile of 23 and a standard score of 91) is sufficient to consider a child at risk. A *TRI* of 8 (i.e., a percentile of 11 and a standard score of 78) is sufficient to consider a child to demonstrate severe atypical behavioral dysfunction using the –1.5 *SD* cutoff. We suggest that professionals use the TABS *TRI* score to justify a diagnosis of temperament/regulatory disorder consistent with Global Assessment of Functioning in the DSM-IV (APA, 1994).

Vignettes Illustrating the Use of TABS

The following vignettes portray problems in temperament and self-regulatory behavior of two young children, one at risk for atypical development and one with ASD. These vignettes illustrate 1) completed TABS Assessment Tools, 2) comparisons of TABS with other developmental measures, and 3) examples of the use of TABS in early intervention. Each vignette contains an overview of the child's problem, a completed TABS Assessment Tool, intervention targets based on TABS, and a TABS Assessment Tool completed subsequent to intervention.

Brent: A Child without Developmental Delays but at Risk for Atypical Development

Brent Walker had been a concern to his parents since infancy. Brent's parents were sure he was smart, although he was very frustrating. As an infant, he was colicky and resistant to breast feeding, and he had trouble sleeping, spit up food, had tantrums, and cried inconsolably. Once he began walking, he became even more difficult; consequently, his parents brought him to a child development center for a developmental assessment. At 18 months, Brent showed high-average developmental skills on the Bayley Scales of Infant Development (Bayley, 1969), scoring a developmental age of 22 months. He talked in two- and three-word phrases, completed puzzles, and remembered many things that he saw on television or was told; however, he seldom complied with requests, never seemed to stop moving, and was easily upset by changes. Brent's mother completed a TABS Assessment Tool, and Figure 3.3 shows the Results section from the last page of the completed Assessment Tool. Because 18 items were checked *Yes,* Brent's behavior was considered highly atypical. His *TRI* score was below the first percentile. Moreover, Mrs. Walker indicated she needed help with (the same) 18 items that she had checked. Figure 3.4 shows the specific TABS items that were checked *Yes* and *Need Help* by Mrs. Walker.

Because Brent's testing did not indicate developmental delay which would qualify him for services, his difficult behavior was likely to continue without intervention. The Walkers were then advised to obtain early intervention services on their own. They entered Brent in a toddler play group,

	Raw Scores	Percentile	Standard Score (or T-score)
Detached	1	23	47
Hyper-sensitive/active	13	<1	<15
Underreactive	0	60	54
Dysregulated	4	<1	4
Temperament & Regulatory Index (TRI) (total of four factor raw scores)	18	<1	<51

Figure 3.3. Brent's normative TABS levels at the start of services.

DETACHED	No	Yes	Need Help
1. Consistently upset by changes in schedule	☐	☒	☒
2. Emotions don't match what is going on	☒	☐	☐
3. Seems to look through or past people	☒	☐	☐
4. Resists looking you in the eye	☒	☐	☐
5. Acts like others are not there	☒	☐	☐
6. Hardly ever starts on own to play with others	☒	☐	☐
7. Moods and wants are too hard to figure out	☒	☐	☐
8. Seems to be in "own world"	☒	☐	☐
9. Often stares into space	☒	☐	☐
10. "Tunes out," loses contact with what is going on	☒	☐	☐
11. Plays with toys in strange ways	☒	☐	☐
12. Plays with toys as if confused by how they work	☒	☐	☐
13. Makes strange throat noises	☒	☐	☐
14. Disturbed by too much light, noise, or touching	☒	☐	☐
15. Overexcited in crowded places	☒	☐	☐
16. Stares at lights	☒	☐	☐
17. Overly interested in toy/object	☒	☐	☐
18. Flaps hands over and over	☒	☐	☐
19. Shakes head over and over	☒	☐	☐
20. Wanders around without purpose	☒	☐	☐
Detached Raw Score →		1	

HYPER-SENSITIVE/ACTIVE	No	Yes	Need Help
21. Upset by every little thing	☐	☒	☒
22. Often difficult to soothe when upset and crying	☐	☒	☒
23. Has wide swings in mood	☐	☒	☒
24. Gets angry too easily	☐	☒	☒
25. Too easily frustrated	☐	☒	☒
26. Has wild temper tantrums	☐	☒	☒
27. Frequently irritable, "touchy," or fussy	☐	☒	☒
28. Can't wait at all for food or toy	☐	☒	☒
29. Demands attention continually	☒	☐	☐
30. Controls adult's behavior, "is the boss"	☐	☒	☒

Figure 3.4. Brent's reported regulatory difficulties. *(continued)*

Figure 3.4. *(continued)*

	No	Yes	Need Help
31. Jealous too often	X		
32. Mostly on the go, "in high gear"		X	X
33. Doesn't sit still		X	X
34. Too "grabby," impulsive		X	X
35. Almost always refuses to do what is told		X	X
36. Throws or breaks things on purpose	X		
37. Bites, hits, kicks others	X		
Hyper-sensitive/active Raw Score →		13	

DYSREGULATED	No	Yes	Need Help
49. Often cries too long		X	X
50. Often frightened by dreams or the nighttime	X		
51. Screams in sleep and can't be comforted	X		
52. Can't comfort self when upset		X	X
53. Wakes up often and doesn't fall back asleep		X	X
54. Doesn't have a regular sleep schedule	X		
55. Too often needs help to fall asleep		X	X
Dysregulated Raw Score →		4	

and his teacher received behavioral support from the early intervention program. That program also provided behavioral support to Brent's parents at home, teaching them to manage his behavior, to defuse situations that might lead to tantrums, and to accommodate his idiosyncrasies. Specifically, Brent's teacher, mother, and therapeutic support staff person applied the interventions described in Chapter 7 to several of the areas in which Mrs. Walker indicated she needed help. In Table 3.1, these interventions are cross-referenced to Brent's behavior.

Table 3.1. Interventions for Brent

Need help item		Intervention (Chapter 7)
21	Upset by every little thing	Desensitization, reinforcement
23	Has wide swings in mood	Modeling in play, reinforcement
25	Too easily frustrated	Interruption, incompatible activities
26	Has wild temper tantrums	Desensitization, planned ignoring
27	Frequently irritable, "touchy," or fussy	Desensitization, reinforcement of incompatible behavior
28	Can't wait at all for food or toy	Delay, modeling, reinforcement
35	Almost always refuses to do what is told	Task completion, modeling, reinforcement

	Raw Scores	Percentile	Standard Score (or T-score)
Detached	0	65	55
Hyper-sensitive/active	3	22	44
Underreactive	0	60	54
Dysregulated	1	15	42
Temperament & Regulatory Index (TRI) (total of four factor raw scores)	4	28	95

Figure 3.5. Brent's improvements in self-regulatory behavior on the TABS Assessment Tool after 12 months of services.

As shown in Figure 3.5, after 12 months of integrated home and center-based services, Brent's problem behaviors decreased substantially, although he remained difficult and demanding. Even though he no longer met eligibility criteria, the early intervention program continued to provide consultative services to his parents and Brent's play group teacher.

Phillip: A Child with ASD

Phillip Mertz was 34 months old when his mother enrolled him in an early intervention program. She was concerned that he was not talking and had difficulty playing with others. In addition, he seemed to "get stuck on" certain play activities, such as lining up toy cars in rows and repeatedly viewing specific television shows such as *Wheel of Fortune.* He would become very upset and have tantrums if removed from these activities.

For several months, Phillip's teacher and speech-language pathologist at the early intervention program worked with him and his mother to increase his language, his knowledge of toys, and his ability to play with others, yet Phillip's behavior continued to be challenging. He often wandered about the room, flapped his hands when upset, mixed single words while pointing and squealing to communicate, and had tantrums when moving from one situation to another.

At the end of the school year, Phillip was reevaluated by a multidisciplinary team in preparation for revising his IFSP. Table 3.2 shows Phillip's developmental levels which were derived from the Early Intervention De-

Table 3.2. Phillip's developmental levels at 43 months

Domain	Developmental age (DA)	Developmental quotient (DQ)
Cognitive	18 months	50
Language	12 months	34
Social-emotional	9 months	26
Perceptual/fine motor	21 months	60
Gross motor	32 months	91
Self-care	23 months	66

velopmental Profile (Rogers & D'Eugenio, 1981), Preschool Language Scale (Zimmermann, Steiner, & Pond, 1979), and Family Support Scale (Dunst, Jenkins, & Trivette, 1988). Clearly, Phillip demonstrated marked delays in all areas.

Both the early childhood specialists and Phillip's parents suspected that Phillip had a problem more complicated than a general developmental delay. They became concerned that Phillip showed a pattern of behavior and developmental characteristics associated with PDD. The Mertzes brought Phillip to a university-affiliated hospital. They hoped to find a specific diagnosis in order to increase the intensity and focus of Phillip's programs in the coming year. Initially, Mrs. Mertz completed a TABS Screener that is shown in Figure 3.6. Phillip's raw score of 6 was a clear indication that a full TABS Assessment Tool should be completed.

The hospital staff observed Phillip at home and in the preschool for 3 days to gain an independent understanding of his behavior. Mrs. Mertz then completed a TABS Assessment Tool. She indicated 1 problem in the *Hyper-sensitive/active* subtest and 1 problem in the *Dysregulated* subtest; however, she indicated 10 problems in the *Detached* subtest and 5 problems

	No	Yes
1. Emotions don't match what is going on	[X]	[ ]
2. Gets angry too easily	[X]	[ ]
3. Too easily frustrated	[X]	[ ]
4. Has wild temper tantrums	[X]	[ ]
5. Frequently irritable, "touchy," or fussy	[X]	[ ]
6. Can't comfort self when upset	[X]	[ ]
7. Doesn't pay attention to sights and sounds	[X]	[ ]
8. Seems to look through or past people	[ ]	[X]
9. Resists looking you in the eye	[ ]	[X]
10. Too "grabby," impulsive	[X]	[ ]
11. Moods and wants are too hard to figure out	[ ]	[X]
12. Seems to be in "own world"	[ ]	[X]
13. "Tunes out," loses contact with what is going on	[ ]	[X]
14. Overexcited in crowded places	[X]	[ ]
15. Wanders around without purpose	[ ]	[X]

III. RESULTS

Add all the items marked *Yes* and place the total in the box below labeled Raw Score. A score of 1 or 2 indicates that the child may be at risk for atypical development and self-regulatory behavior. A score of 3 or more indicates that the child's temperament and self-regulatory behavior are probably atypical for his or her age. Follow-up with a complete 55-item TABS Assessment Tool is recommended for any score other than 0.

Raw Score [6]   Recommended for follow up with TABS Assessment Tool: Yes [X] No [ ]

Figure 3.6. TABS Screener on Phillip.

DETACHED	No	Yes	Need Help
1. Consistently upset by changes in schedule	☐	☒	☒
2. Emotions don't match what is going on	☒	☐	☐
3. Seems to look through or past people	☐	☒	☐
4. Resists looking you in the eye	☐	☒	☒
5. Acts like others are not there	☐	☒	☐
6. Hardly ever starts on own to play with others	☐	☒	☒
7. Moods and wants are too hard to figure out	☒	☐	☐
8. Seems to be in "own world"	☐	☒	☒
9. Often stares into space	☐	☒	☐
10. "Tunes out," loses contact with what is going on	☒	☐	☐
11. Plays with toys in strange ways	☐	☒	☒
12. Plays with toys as if confused by how they work	☒	☐	☐
13. Makes strange throat noises	☒	☐	☐
14. Disturbed by too much light, noise, or touching	☒	☐	☐
15. Overexcited in crowded places	☒	☐	☐
16. Stares at lights	☒	☐	☐
17. Overly interested in toy/object	☐	☒	☒
18. Flaps hands over and over	☐	☒	☒
19. Shakes head over and over	☒	☐	☐
20. Wanders around without purpose	☒	☐	☐
Detached Raw Score →		10	

Figure 3.7. Phillip's *Detached* TABS ratings.

in the *Underreactive* subtest. Her ratings for these last two subtests are shown in Figures 3.7 and 3.8, respectively. Many of Mrs. Mertz's responses were consistent with her prior reports of Phillip's problem behavior (e.g., being upset by changes in routine, self-stimulatory behavior, problems playing with other children); however, she indicated additional problems when she completed the TABS Assessment Tool (e.g., trouble maintaining eye contact, hyposensitivity to sounds and other stimulation, not responding consistently when his name was called). As shown in Figure 3.9, Phillip's TABS Results indicate just how unusual was the number of difficulties he had in general—his *TRI* was below the first percentile; moreover, his difficulties were concentrated in the areas of detachment and underactivity. It also seems apparent that Mrs. Mertz sought help for most of the problems checked.

Phillip was then assessed using the Childhood Autism Rating Scale (Schopler, 1986); his score of 42 indicated severe difficulties in similar behaviors and suggested a diagnosis of ASD. Subsequently, Phillip was assessed with the DSM-IV Autism Checklist (APA, 1994); his score of 9 was consistent with a diagnosis of ASD.

UNDERREACTIVE	No	Yes	Need Help
38. Rarely smiles, giggles, or laughs at funny things	☐	☒	☒
39. Doesn't pay attention to sights and sounds	☐	☒	☒
40. Doesn't seem to watch moving objects	☒	☐	☐
41. Shows no surprise to new events	☐	☒	☒
42. Doesn't react to own name	☐	☒	☒
43. Doesn't care when others are hurt	☒	☐	☐
44. Doesn't play much at all	☒	☐	☐
45. Doesn't enjoy playing with mother or caregiver	☐	☒	☒
46. Isn't upset when toy is taken away	☒	☐	☐
47. Almost never babbles or tries to talk	☒	☐	☐
48. Doesn't react to sounds	☒	☐	☐
Underreactive Raw Score →		5	

Figure 3.8. Phillip's *Underreactive* TABS ratings.

	Raw Scores	Percentile	Standard Score (or T-score)
Detached	10	<1	0
Hyper-sensitive/active	1	46	53
Underreactive	5	<1	<7
Dysregulated	1	15	42
Temperament & Regulatory Index (TRI) (total of four factor raw scores)	17	<1	<51

Figure 3.9. Phillip's normative TABS levels before transition and intervention.

Table 3.3. Interventions for Phillip

Need help item		Intervention (Chapter 7)
4	Resists looking you in eye	Physical prompts
17	Overly interested in toy/object	Prompts, modeling in play
18	Flaps hands over and over	Interruption, incompatible activities
22	Often difficult to soothe when upset and crying	Desensitization, planned ignoring
42	Doesn't react to own name	Cuing, reinforcement
54	Doesn't have a regular sleep schedule	Sleep routine, record, and procedures

Specific interventions, described in Chapter 7, were recommended for inclusion in Phillip's revised IEP. These recommendations included highly structured programming for 5 days per week in one-to-one settings (see Table 3.3). In addition, his IEP provided for inclusion with typical peers, development of a communications system, and parent training and involvement in the program. After 12 months of services, when Phillip was 48 months old, he received much lower TABS ratings, although there were still significant problems (see Figure 3.10). Teachers also reported simultaneous increases in Phillip's language and social behaviors.

	Raw Scores	Percentile	Standard Score (or T-score)
Detached	4	3	23
Hyper-sensitive/active	2	32	48
Underreactive	2	6	31
Dysregulated	1	15	42
Temperament & Regulatory Index (TRI) (total of four factor raw scores)	9	8	73

Figure 3.10. Phillip's normative TABS levels after 12 months of intervention.

4

TABS Development

ITEM DEVELOPMENT

A series of studies from 1988 to 1998 greatly assisted in TABS item development as well as conceptual and format refinement. An exploratory item pool was assembled based on clinical impressions, discussions with colleagues, and a cursory review of relevant literature. Referred to as the Baby Atypical Behavior Inventory (BABI), the initial index covered an age range of 12–36 months. Following some limited use of BABI, Amos (1986) conducted a comprehensive review of the literature in child psychopathology. Her review included major journals and texts relevant to early childhood atypical behavior and resulted in descriptions of behaviors, related syndromes, and possible treatment approaches for each item (atypical behavior) identified through the search. The thoroughness of the literature research provided a major foundation for the TABS item pool available for normative and psychometric studies.

Capone (1988) conducted a retrospective study in which parents of children enrolled in elementary school were asked to complete a 152-item Atypical Infant and Toddler Behavior Questionnaire (AITBQ) based on research by Amos (1986) and Capone (1988) as well as unpublished research by the TABS authors. One parent group ($N = 171$) had children enrolled in the general education program within their school districts. The other parent group ($N = 222$) had children enrolled in special education programs within the same school districts. The samples were comparable in terms of critical demographics. Both groups were asked to complete the AITBQ, requiring recollection of their children as infants, from birth to 3 years old. Primary school children enrolled in special education evidenced a significantly higher number of atypical behaviors, as reported by parents. One analysis, for example, revealed that, using questionnaire results, the percentage of parents' responses correctly classifying special education versus general education placement was 85%. Although the problems of retrospective research are acknowledged (and discussed by Capone), the strong relationship between the questionnaire items and educational placement gave great impetus and direction in our efforts to further refine the item pool for TABS.

Research by Vacca (1995) was revealing in its analysis of existing materials available for early childhood appraisal. Through a survey of school psychologists responsible for assessing infants and preschoolers, several findings provided further support for the development of TABS. One major finding was that numerous behaviors exhibited by infants and young children with neurological disabilities (e.g., prenatal drug exposure, acquired brain injury, other recognized syndromes) are not assessed by conventional measures. Specifically, psychologists reported that the measures they used for eligibility determination were not adequate for detecting the presence of atypical behaviors, such as hand flapping, excessive staring at bright lights, body rocking (behaviors included in TABS). Consistent with his survey research, Vacca cited related research that underscores the absence on developmental measures of items related to excessive docility or irritability, sleep disturbances, and problems in consolability. Also noted as not captured in testing situations are children's abilities to cope with daily challenges, to adapt to circumstances, and to initiate changes in the environment to meet their needs. Furthermore, deviant or seriously atypical behaviors may not be exhibited during decontextualized standardized assessment sessions. Demands of the child's at-home or preschool situation, however, may occasion behaviors that can be reported by parents and professionals who spend time with the child in these contexts. Implications for TABS were clear: It seemed important that TABS be designed to capture the judgments of people familiar with the child, providing a wider sampling of child functioning based on accumulated impressions, as opposed to a narrow sampling through limited observations during a structured assessment session. Among Vacca's (1995) conclusions from the survey research was that there is a need for measures of atypical behavior as evidenced by children in their natural environments and that available developmental instruments were not responsive to this need.

In a study by Banks (1997), a panel of experts was employed to analyze item content of commonly used developmental assessment materials. Protocols were analyzed by obtaining a frequency count of items that were judged to address atypical behavior. Experts also analyzed the relationship between items and the several developmental domains. Results of the analysis by a panel of experts converge with findings of the Vacca (1995) study: The instruments typically used for infant and early childhood assessment do not address the detection of atypical behaviors that may have serious developmental outcomes.

Taken collectively, the studies cited in this section are consistent with the general literature on early childhood assessment. Both previous research and TABS research and field testing are consistent in showing the importance of early detection of atypical behavior.

Preliminary Steps in Item Selection

To simplify data entry and analysis, the original item pool (k = 154) was used in all field tests and standardization studies, although it was soon apparent that only about one third to one half of the items would have the necessary statistical characteristics to be retained in the final version of TABS. Once the data had been collected and entered, the final sample of items was selected using a combination of univariate and multivariate statistical procedures.

Preliminary analyses, based on different samples of children with varying degrees of disability, suggested two different factor structures. In all cases, the first two factors were robust. The lower the percentage of children with disabilities in the sample, however, the more likely was a three-factor solution; the greater the percentage of children with disabilities in the sample, the more likely was a four-factor solution.[1] To determine the final items to be included in TABS, we used all of the data from all 949 of the children who had been assessed.

First, we created seven composite scores: the total of all items, the total for each of the four sets of items believed to represent the four factors underlying TABS, the sum of those four subtests, and the sum of items that did not load on any of the four subtests. Next, we calculated a series of point biserial correlation coefficients between each of the 154 items and the seven composite scores. Sixty-five items had a point biserial coefficient equal to or greater than .375 with at least one of the seven composites; these items were retained for subsequent factor analyses.

Principal components factor analysis with varimax rotation of the 65 items revealed a complex factor structure; however, a four-factor solution proved statistically and theoretically interpretable for three reasons. First, although 14 factors had Eigenvalues of 1 or more, a scree plot of the first six values (i.e., 11.74, 4.37, 2.22, 2.01, 1.73, 1.42) suggested a logical break between factors 4 and 5. Second, only four factors accounted for 5% or more of the rotated variance, with the fourth factor accounting for 5.19%. Third, the four-factor solution was quite similar to ones found earlier with various subsamples and was consistent with the logic of other researchers and clinicians (ZERO TO THREE, 1994). Therefore, we committed to the four-factor solution. We then examined the factor loadings of individual items. Three items had loadings of less than .375 on any factor, so these items were dropped from the item pool.

Final Steps in Item Selection

The characteristics of the remaining 62 items were examined as a function of age, sex, and severity of disability of the 833 children in the norm samples. This analysis was complicated by the fact that there were different numbers of boys and girls at each age and by the fact that there were different percentages of boys and girls with disabilities at each age. In order to weight these item means (*p*-values) equally by these demographic variables, four values for each item at each age were calculated: the *p* for boys with disabilities, the *p* for girls with disabilities, the *p* for boys believed to be not at risk, and the *p* for girls believed to be not at risk. The four *p*-values were

[1]This finding is quite consistent with the theoretical formulations underlying DC:0–3 classifications of regulatory disorders.

averaged for each age (across sex and disability), for sex (across age and disability), and for disability (across age and sex). The overwhelming majority of these *p*-values showed only random fluctuation between males and females and among whole-year age groups. Most items showed substantial increases across the three risk levels. Seven items showed pronounced swings over age or undesirable progression over severity of disability. These seven items were dropped; thus, the final item pool consisted of 55 items.

The 55-Item TABS Assessment Tool

Because we were not concerned with the effect of age or outliers on factor analyses, we used the data from 949 subjects (833 subjects plus 116 children who were too old to be included in the norms or whose scores were more than 3 *SD*s from the mean) to verify the presence of four factors and to use these factor loadings as a basis for naming the factors; therefore, a principal components factor analysis was performed. Eleven factors with Eigenvalues greater than 1 were found. A scree plot of these Eigenvalues indicated a break between factors 4 and 5 (see Figure 4.1). In addition, the four rotated factors accounted for 5% or more of the total variance, with the fourth factor accounting for 5.01%. Thus, a four-factor solution for 55 items seemed not only parsimonious but also theoretically meaningful.

The factor loadings for each item are shown in Table 4.1. Considering the factor loadings and the behaviors sampled by each item, we named

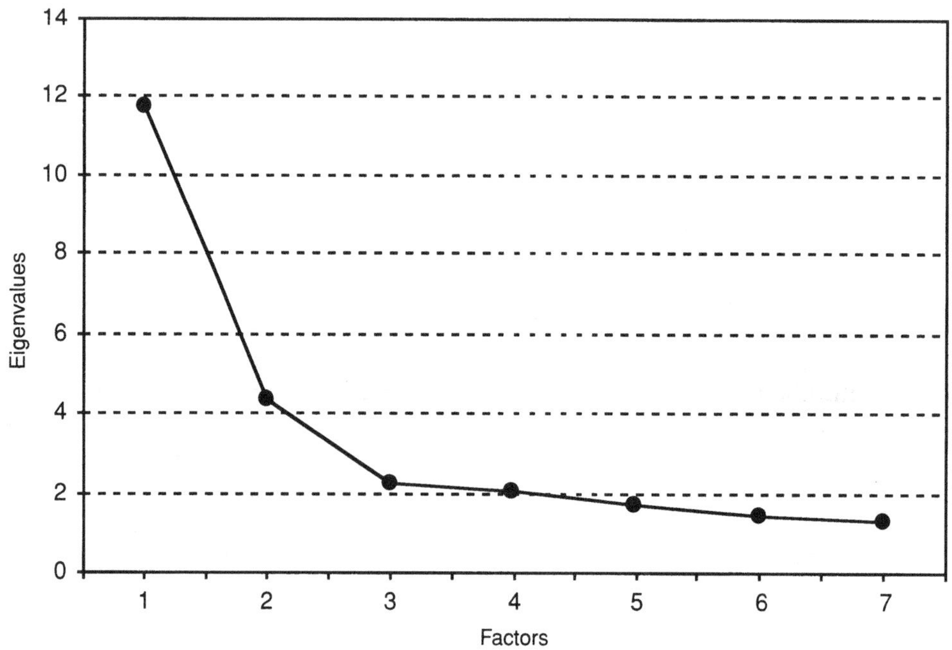

Figure 4.1. Scree plot of the Eigenvalues of the first seven factors.

Table 4.1. Correlations between the 55 items and each TABS factor

Item	F1 (*k*=20) *11.63	F2 (*k*=17) *11.66	F3 (*k*=11) *8.66	F4 (*k*=7) *5.02
1	**0.39**	0.37	0.05	0.12
2	**0.47**	0.20	0.20	0.12
3	**0.61**	0.11	0.30	0.12
4	**0.50**	0.18	0.22	0.12
5	**0.57**	0.18	0.28	0.04
6	**0.44**	0.12	0.40	0.02
7	**0.40**	0.38	0.26	0.07
8	**0.67**	0.10	0.30	0.03
9	**0.56**	−0.02	0.28	0.24
10	**0.60**	0.15	0.23	0.10
11	**0.52**	0.05	0.11	−0.05
12	**0.40**	0.09	0.34	−0.04
13	**0.40**	0.14	0.07	0.14
14	**0.50**	0.16	0.01	0.10
15	**0.52**	0.34	−0.04	0.08
16	**0.56**	−0.04	0.10	0.22
17	**0.59**	0.12	0.15	−0.11
18	**0.49**	0.11	0.12	−0.02
19	**0.42**	0.06	0.05	0.12
20	**0.56**	0.18	0.20	−0.09
21	0.11	**0.54**	0.07	0.14
22	0.29	**0.39**	−0.01	0.34
23	0.31	**0.55**	−0.04	0.12
24	0.09	**0.70**	0.05	0.09
25	0.26	**0.64**	−0.04	0.08
26	0.16	**0.62**	0.01	0.17
27	0.23	**0.47**	0.05	0.33
28	0.20	**0.57**	0.14	0.07
29	0.02	**0.54**	0.10	0.18
30	−0.01	**0.54**	0.01	0.16
31	−0.08	**0.51**	0.11	0.04
32	0.14	**0.53**	0.13	0.04
33	0.23	**0.54**	0.14	−0.02
34	0.11	**0.68**	0.07	0.03
35	0.06	**0.58**	0.10	0.05
36	0.12	**0.51**	0.03	0.03
37	0.07	**0.52**	0.04	0.01
38	0.16	−0.02	**0.48**	0.06
39	0.31	0.11	**0.56**	0.14
40	0.09	0.01	**0.58**	0.14
41	0.26	0.05	**0.63**	0.01
42	0.31	0.06	**0.67**	0.06
43	0.21	0.16	**0.54**	−0.02
44	0.21	−0.08	**0.63**	0.06
45	0.04	0.12	**0.64**	−0.10
46	−0.02	0.18	**0.46**	0.07
47	0.12	0.04	**0.53**	0.03
48	0.14	0.04	**0.61**	0.13

continued

Table 4.1. *(continued)*

Item	F1 (*k*=20) *11.63	F2 (*k*=17) *11.66	F3 (*k*=11) *8.66	F4 (*k*=7) *5.02
49	0.14	0.37	−0.01	**0.42**
50	0.01	0.07	0.06	**0.49**
51	−0.04	0.14	0.06	**0.54**
52	0.26	0.32	0.08	**0.47**
53	0.28	0.08	−0.02	**0.61**
54	0.05	0.16	0.20	**0.60**
55	0.07	0.09	0.07	**0.62**

Key: * = % Total S^2

factor 1 *Detached,* factor 2 *Hyper-sensitive/active,* factor 3 *Underreactive,* and factor 4 *Dysregulated.*

Selecting Items for the TABS Screener

Because many practitioners are interested in screening large numbers of children quickly and effectively, we developed a TABS Screener. The Screener consists of 15 TABS items that are reliable and that accurately predict the *Temperament and Regulatory Index* (*TRI*). We used three criteria to select screener items: 1) items had to correlate highly with the *TRI,* 2) items had to correlate with the Screener raw score, and 3) items had to show large differences between children with and without disabilities. Items 2, 3, 4, 7, 8, 10, 15, 20, 24, 25, 26, 27, 34, 39, and 52 met these criteria.

The ability of the TABS Screener to identify children who are at risk is demonstrated by its high predictive validity. Approximately 83% of children are correctly classified by the Screener. Only 2.4% of the decisions result in false negatives (children who are indeed at risk but who are classified on the Screener as not in need of further assessment); about 14.5% of the decisions result in false positives (children who are not in need of further assessment but who are classified on the Screener as needing further assessment).

NORMS

Sampling Procedures

One fundamental assumption shaped the development of norms for TABS. We believed that the atypical behaviors being assessed were essentially unrelated to socioeconomic class, geographic factors, sex, and ethnic or cultural identity. Rather, we consider the behaviors sampled by TABS as symptomatic of or closely associated with a variety of known syndromes or neurologically based disorders that are considered aberrant in any social class, geographic area, and cultural group. Consequently, there was no need to obtain precisely representative normative samples of children without disabilities.

A sample of children not identified as having disabilities was necessary to provide norms for TABS, to estimate the prevalence of the behaviors assessed by the scale in the population without disabilities, and to provide information about the validity of TABS. A sample of children with disabilities was also needed for validating TABS. The nature of TABS items (i.e., highly aberrant behavior) presumed a substantially higher prevalence among populations with disabilities. Moreover, the statistical analyses needed to validate TABS required that the children's performances vary on each item (i.e., the items have variance); however, if the items were indeed valid, there should be little or no variation on each item for children without disabilities. Sufficient item variance could be ensured only by using a sample of children with disabilities or a pooled sample of children with and without disabilities.

Children came from a variety of agencies and organizations serving children with and without disabilities. For 5 years, almost 200 sites participated in our data collection, field trials, and norming efforts. Agencies in 33 states and 3 Canadian provinces are included in the effort, covering all pertinent geographic and socioeconomic circumstances.

These children were divided into two samples. The first sample was composed of children with disabilities. The second sample was composed of children who were considered as not having disabilities. It is important to note that some of the children without disabilities came from hospital and clinic referrals; however, the problems that these children were experiencing were not of a nature that would have required identifying them with a disability.

Selecting a Normative Sample of Children without Disabilities

Protocols were completed for a total of 758 children; however, 45 children were dropped because their protocols did not contain their ages. An additional 58 children were dropped because they were outside the target age range: 39 children were younger than 11 months old, and 19 children were 72 months or older. Thus, 655 children remained in the sample.

The distribution of TABS scores of the children without disabilities was then examined for outliers. We were concerned about the possibility that children with disabilities were included in the sample of children believed to be typical. The overwhelming majority of these students were not necessarily diagnosed as being typical; rather, they had simply not been classified as having disabilities. Thus, in inclusive agencies it was quite possible for a child with a disability to be served without being labeled; therefore, we calculated means and standard deviations of TABS scores for children not at risk. Of the 655 children, 34 had total scores that were more than 3 *SD*s above the mean and were considered outliers; these children were dropped from the normative group, and the normative sample was reduced to 621 children.

Characteristics of the Normative Sample

The normative sample was composed of 621 children between 11 and 71 months of age. About half (52%) of the sample were 2 years old or younger. All data were collected and provided to us without identifying information to protect the anonymity of the children and their families. Unfortunately, information about the child's sex was omitted in about 60% of the cases. As shown in Table 4.2, when known, the sex of the children was distributed quite evenly between boys (53%) and girls (47%).

Table 4.2. Age and sex distribution of TABS normative sample ($N = 621$)

Age (in years)	*n*	Male	Female	Not recorded
1	120	18	25	77
2	203	23	15	165
3	83	21	16	46
4	161	49	41	71
5	54	19	11	24

TABS Performance of Normative Sample

The mean and standard deviation of TABS scores for boys and girls are shown in Table 4.3. Mean differences between sexes are not significant; the correlations between sex and each TABS score never exceeded .07 and were not significant at the .30 level of probability.

Descriptive statistics by age for the raw scores of children without disabilities on each TABS composite are shown in Table 4.4. As is apparent from these data, score distributions are generally skewed, and hyper-sensitive/active behavior is more common than detached, underreactive, or dysregulated behavior.

First, we investigated the correlation between each score and age. The correlation between age and *TRI* ($r = -.07$) for the 621 children was not significant at the .10 level of probability. The results for *Detached, Hyper-sensitive/active, Underreactive* and *Dysregulated* were similar; correlations with age ($r = .041$, .003, –.13, and –.09, respectively) were not statistically significant. We also conducted a series of one-way analyses of variance to compare the TABS scores at each age. Overall, F-tests were not significant—(.05) for three scores: *TRI, Detached,* and *Dysregulated.* The overall F-test was significant for *Hyper-sensitive/active,* but none of the follow-up comparisons using the Tukey HSD procedure were significant at the .05 level. The overall F-test was also significant for *Underreactive:* One individual comparison (age 1 = age 4) was statistically significant (.05). Together, these results indicate that there are no systematic and orderly differences among ages for any of the TABS scores; consequently, there is no need to develop interpretative norms for separate ages.

Characteristics of the Sample of Children with Disabilities

Although TABS items are widely regarded as being associated with or indicative of a variety of disabilities, the frequency of these behaviors in popula-

Table 4.3. TABS means and standard deviations by sex

Sample	TRI	Detached	Hyper-sensitive/ active	Under- reactive	Dys- regulated
Boys ($n = 130$)					
M	3.07	0.66	1.88	0.25	0.28
SD	3.35	1.25	2.20	0.76	0.66
Girls ($n = 108$)					
M	2.94	0.60	1.68	0.28	0.38
SD	3.60	1.16	2.28	0.88	0.90

Table 4.4. TABS means and standard deviations, by age, for children classified as not having disabilities

Sample	TRI	Detached	Hyper-sensitive/ active	Under- reactive	Dys- regulated
1-year-olds (*n* = 120)					
M	2.97	0.58	1.38	0.58	0.42
SD	3.29	1.16	2.01	1.04	0.87
2-year-olds (*n* = 203)					
M	3.26	0.74	1.74	0.36	0.41
SD	3.61	1.38	2.22	0.84	0.92
3-year-olds (*n* = 83)					
M	3.43	0.75	2.12	0.30	0.26
SD	3.64	1.33	2.50	0.76	0.59
4-year-olds (*n* = 161)					
M	2.37	0.51	1.34	0.24	0.29
SD	3.01	1.19	1.76	0.74	0.68
5-year-olds (*n* = 54)					
M	2.76	0.52	1.78	0.22	0.24
SD	3.44	1.02	2.33	0.77	0.55
Overall (*N* = 621)					
M	2.95	0.63	1.62	0.35	0.35
SD	3.40	1.26	2.13	0.85	0.79

tions of children with disabilities is not known; therefore, we also collected TABS data on 212 children who had been classified as having disabilities independent of their performances on TABS. The performances of these children brought additional data to bear on the interpretation of TABS scores of the nonidentified children.

The sample of children with disabilities ranged from 11 to 71 months of age. Children were labeled as having a disability if they were already classified as having a severe speech, language, or articulation problem. For our purposes, children with only mild speech, language, or articulation problems were not classified as having disabilities. Classified as having disabilities were children with a diagnosis of ADHD, PDD, infantile autism, Aicardi syndrome, brain tumors, cerebral palsy, Down syndrome, Duchenne muscular dystrophy, epilepsy, FAS, fragile X syndrome, severe hearing loss, hyperopia with developmental delay, perinatal hyporia, severe seizure disorders, tuberous sclerosis, velocardiofacial syndrome, and WS. In addition, if a child had been evaluated using the System to Plan Early Childhood Services (Bagnato & Neisworth, 1990) and received a rating of 1 or 2, he or she was classified as having a disability (a rating of 1 or 2 refers to a moderate to severe level of functioning as judged by professional raters).

All data were provided to us without identifying information to protect the anonymity of the children and their families. As shown in Table 4.5, there were about two boys for each girl, although information about the child's sex was omitted in about 15% of the cases. About 55% of the sample were 3 years old or younger.

The TABS means and standard deviations for the total and each subtest of children with disabilities at each age are shown in Table 4.6. *TRI* dis-

Table 4.5. Age and sex distribution of TABS of children with disabilities ($N = 212$)

Age (in years)	*n*	Male	Female	Not recorded
1	31	9	14	8
2	47	25	9	13
3	40	30	8	2
4	72	41	22	9
5	22	17	5	0

tributions are also skewed for this sample, and *Detached* and *Hypersensitive/active* behavior is more common than *Underreactive* and *Dysregulated* behavior. We also conducted a series of one-way analyses of variance to compare TABS scores at each age. Overall F-tests were not significant (.05) for any of the five scores. These results indicate that there are no systematic differences among ages for any of the TABS scores in the sample of children with disabilities.

The five TABS means of the 212 children with disabilities were compared with the TABS means of the 621 children without disabilities. For the total and each subtest, means for the children with disabilities were always significantly ($p < .001$) larger than the means of the children classified as not having disabilities.

SCORES

Derived Scores

Three types of derived scores are provided for TABS users: percentiles, standard scores (*SS*)[2], and standard scores that have been normalized by area transformation (*SS*nd). A percentile rank is an ordinal score that equals the percentage of people who earn the same or a poorer (in this case, higher) raw score; thus, a percentile rank is the percentage of children whose standard score is equal or higher. Percentiles are typically used for decision making and in interpreting results to parents.

A standard score is an equal interval score that indicates a child's performance above or below the mean in standard deviation units. The standard scores for the *TRI* have a mean of 100 and a standard deviation of 15; the standard scores for each subtest have a mean of 50 and a standard deviation of 10. Standard scores are useful when the score is subjected to arithmetic operations (e.g., addition, multiplication). Also, some clinicians prefer standard scores over percentiles.

For some statistical purposes, normal (i.e., bell-shaped or Gaussian) score distributions are preferred. TABS raw scores and standard scores are *not* normally distributed; they are skewed. For those individuals who need or prefer to work with scores that are distributed normally, we have also provided scores that have been normalized by area transformation.

The appendix at the end of the book contains the conversion table. For most purposes, percentiles provide the most useful score for interpreting TABS results to parents or for making educational decisions.

[2]The overall means and standard deviations in Table 4.4 were used in these computations.

Table 4.6. TABS means and standard deviations, by age, for children classified as having disabilities

Sample	TRI	Detached	Hyper-sensitive/ active	Under-reactive	Dys-regulated
1-year-olds (*n* = 31)					
M	12.36	4.19	3.90	2.90	1.36
SD	9.74	4.22	4.25	3.39	1.66
2-year-olds (*n* = 47)					
M	15.94	5.08	7.04	1.94	1.87
SD	10.40	4.67	5.44	2.34	1.93
3-year-olds (*n* = 40)					
M	12.38	4.82	4.75	1.90	0.90
SD	7.76	4.28	4.36	2.05	1.26
4-year-olds (*n* = 72)					
M	13.86	5.21	5.33	2.17	1.15
SD	10.46	4.99	4.19	2.81	1.60
5-year-olds (*n* = 22)					
M	14.04	5.77	5.09	2.04	1.14
SD	10.19	5.25	4.00	2.77	1.49
Overall (*N* = 212)					
M	13.84	5.02	5.37	2.16	1.29
SD	9.85	4.69	4.83	2.67	1.64

Score Interpretation

For TABS, a higher raw score implies a poorer performance; therefore, TABS scores are arranged so that higher derived scores (i.e., percentiles and standard scores) reflect lower raw scores; lower derived scores reflect higher (and more deviant) raw scores.

Although the statistical interpretation of these scores is straightforward, their meaning is not as simple. Given the nature of the items included in TABS (i.e., behaviors that are usually considered atypical), one can argue that any raw score greater than 0 is indicative of some sort of problem. However, such an argument overlooks common experience—typical individuals often exhibit some peculiar behavior some of the time. Recall, also, that most of the behaviors on TABS are not aberrant per se but are considered a developmental concern when their frequency, duration, or intensity is judged to be significantly atypical. An interesting issue in interpreting TABS scores is the question of how many of these atypical behaviors one might reasonably expect children who are developing typically to exhibit. To help answer this question, we constructed a series of figures to depict the overlap of children on each TABS score.

Figures 4.2–4.6 use grouped data to illustrate the overlap of score distributions for typically developing children and children with disabilities. As can be seen in each figure, there is a point [R] where the distributions cross; to the left of that point are lower scores earned more often by typically developing children and to the right of that point are higher scores earned more often by children with disabilities. For example, in Figure 4.2 approximately 75% of typically developing children earn scores to the left

Table 4.7. Classification of children as at risk and having disabilities with TABS scores

	At risk		Disabled	
Measure	Raw Score	Percentile	Raw Score	Percentile
TRI	5	23	10	6
Detached	1	23	3	6
Hyper-sensitive/active	5	9	6	6
Underreactive	1	15	2	6
Dysregulated	1	15	2	5

of that point [i.e., a score of 4 or less] while approximately 74% of children with disabilities earn scores to the right of that point. [i.e., scores of 6 or more]. When a score is equally or more likely to be earned by children with disabilities, that score indicates the child is *at risk* for atypical temperament and/or self-regulation. To the right of point *R*, there is another point [D] that indicates the score awarded to about 6.9% of the typically developing children. Recalling that most of these children have never been clinically evaluated, such an atypical score is considered indicative of a disability. These decision points are summarized in Table 4.7.

Cutoff Scores for the TABS Screener

The TABS Screener is intended to identify students who are suspected of having a disability and require further assessment. To determine what

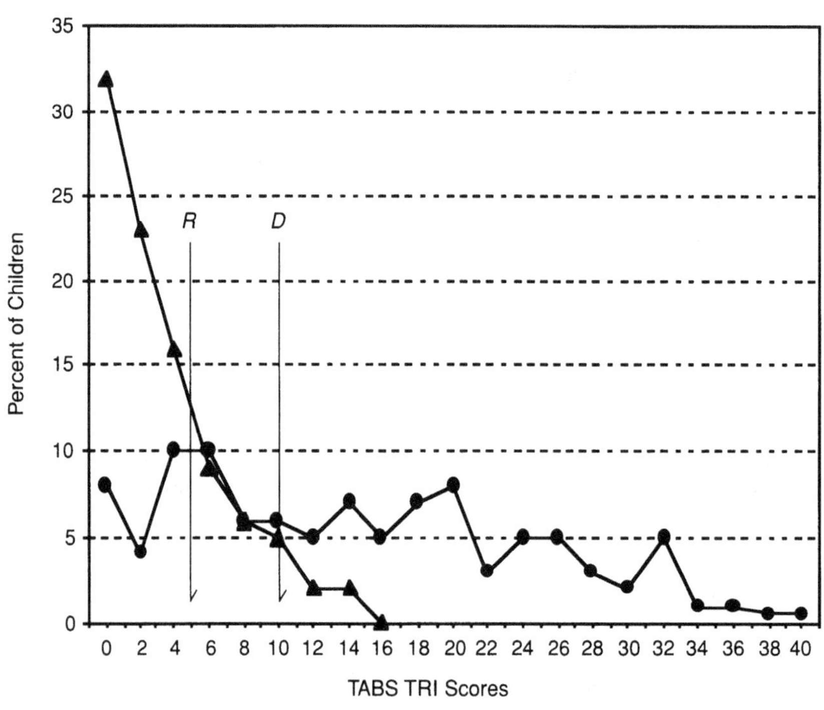

Figure 4.2. Percent of children with and without disabilities in *TRI* ranges. Scores to the right of *R* indicate that the child may be at risk; scores to the right of *D* indicate that the child may have a disability. (Key: ▲, children without disabilities; ●, children with disabilities.)

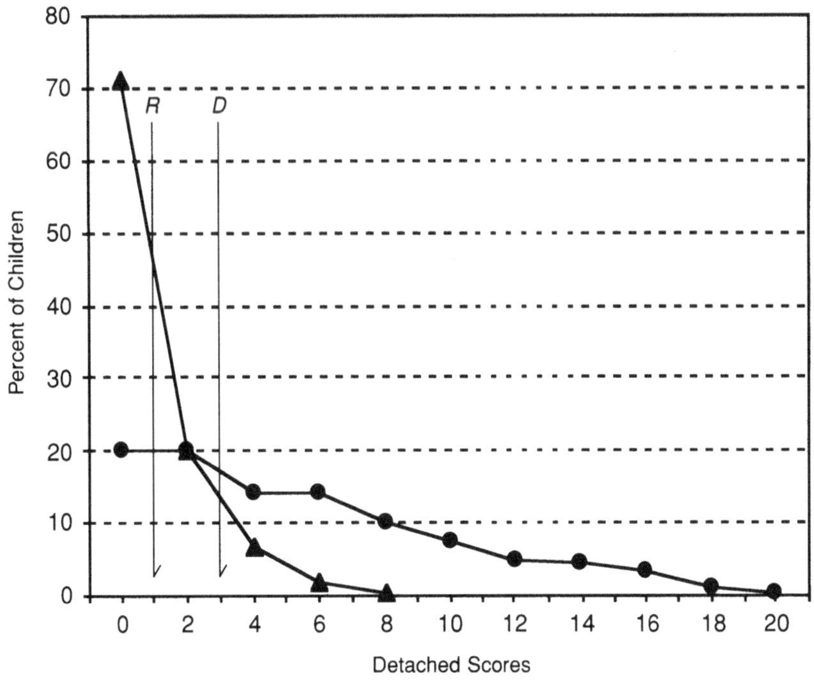

Figure 4.3. Percent of children with and without disabilities in *Detached* score ranges. Scores to the right of *R* indicate that the child may be at risk; scores to the right of *D* indicate that the child may have a disability. (Key: ▲, children without disabilities; ●, children with disabilities.)

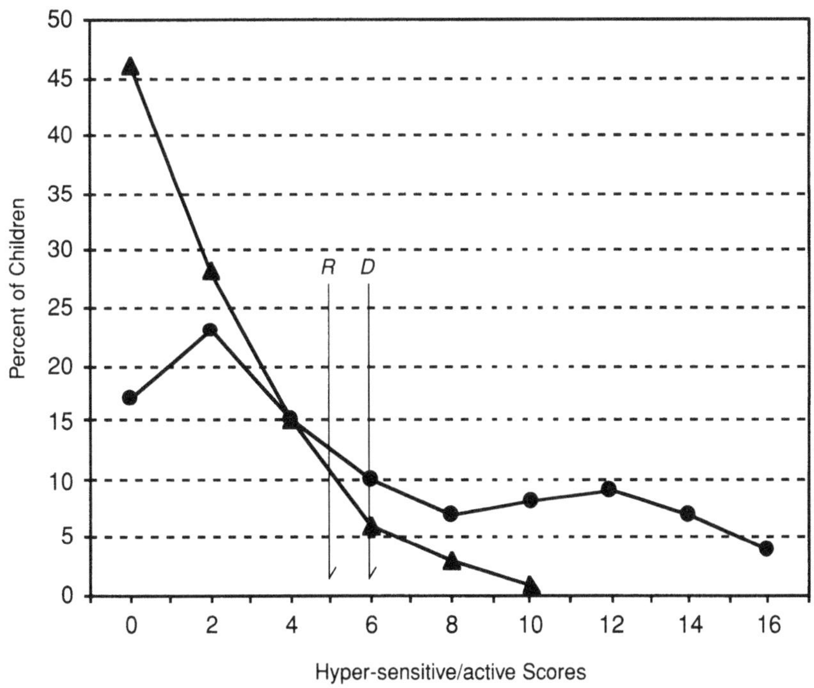

Figure 4.4. Percent of children with and without disabilities in *Hyper-sensitive/active* score ranges. Scores to the right of *R* indicate that the child may be at risk; scores to the right of *D* indicate that the child may have a disability. (Key: ▲, children without disabilities; ●, children with disabilities.)

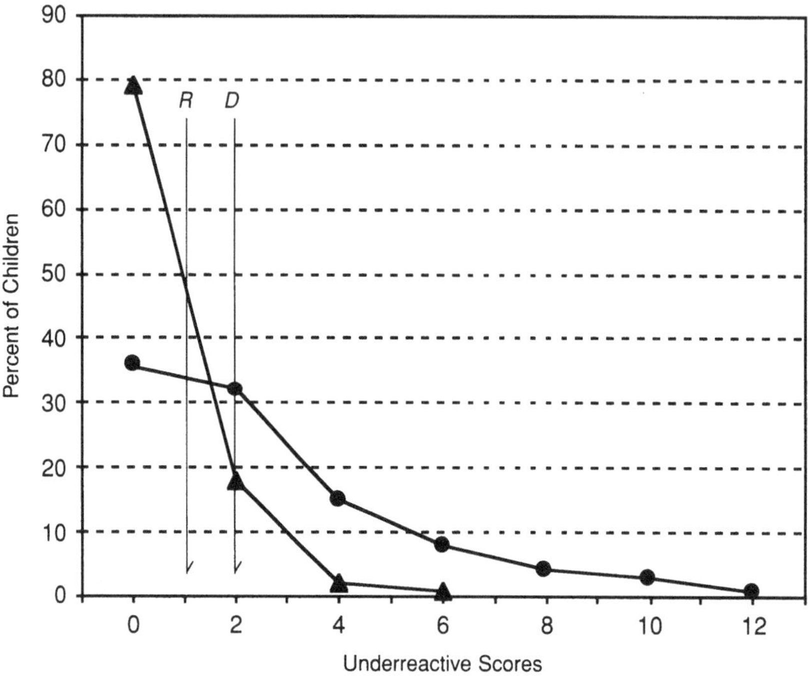

Figure 4.5. Percent of children with and without disabilities in *Underreactive* score ranges. Scores to the right of *R* indicate that the child may be at risk; scores to the right of *D* indicate that the child may have a disability. (Key: ▲, children without disabilities; ●, children with disabilities.)

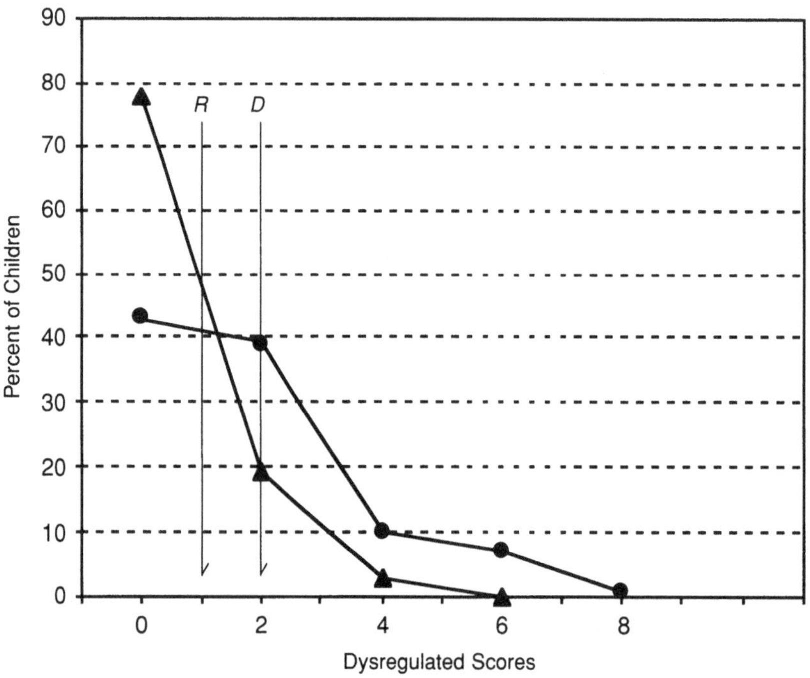

Figure 4.6. Percent of children with and without disabilities in *Dysregulated* score ranges. Scores to the right of *R* indicate that the child may be at risk; scores to the right of *D* indicate that the child may have a disability. (Key: ▲, children without disabilities; ●, children with disabilities.)

Screener scores identify these children, a prediction weight and constant were calculated for predicting a *TRI* from a TABS Screener score. The prediction weight (β) was determined to be 2.62, and the constant (a) was determined to be 1.125; the standard error of estimate was 2.58. These values were then used to predict the *TRI* for each Screener score using the following equation:

$$\text{Predicted } TRI = \beta \cdot \text{TABS Screener Raw Score} + a.$$

*TRI*s are classified as identifying children who are *at risk* when they equal or exceed 5 and as identifying children with disabilities when they equal or exceed 10. A Screener score of 1 predicts a *TRI* of 4, whereas a Screener score of 2 predicts a *TRI* of 6. To minimize the number of false negatives, Screener scores of 1 or 2 classify a child as potentially *at risk.* A Screener score of 3 predicts a *TRI* of 9, whereas a Screener score of 4 predicts a *TRI* of 12. To minimize the number of false negatives, a Screener score of 3 classifies a child as potentially having disabilities.

5

Technical Adequacy of TABS

CONSISTENCY OF TABS SCORES

Reliability is a psychometric term that can refer to consistency of measurement with different but equivalent samples of items. Some authors also use the term to refer to consistency over time (frequently termed *stability* or *test–retest reliability*) and across scorers. In this manual, we use reliability to refer only to consistency of measurement using different, but equivalent, samples of test items.

Internal Consistency

The way in which reliability is estimated depends on whether the test has multiple forms. For tests with a single form, reliability is estimated by an index of internal consistency. We estimated the internal consistency of TABS Assessment Tool scores by correlating equivalent halves of each subtest and the total test. To obtain two halves that represented each subtest more or less equally, we ordered the items by factor loadings within each subtest. Next, we separately summed the odd-numbered items and even-numbered items. We then correlated these two sums for each of TABS' four subtests and the *TRI* (*Temperament & Regulatory Index*, or total raw score) for three different samples: children not believed to be at risk (n = 621), children known to have disabilities (n = 212), and a pooled sample of those two groups (N = 833).

Reliability estimates are directly related to the number of items in the test. Splitting a test or subtest in half systematically underestimates the scale's reliability. Thus, split half correlations are appropriately corrected using a formula developed by Spearman and Brown.[1] Table 5.1 contains these obtained and corrected reliability estimates. As shown in Table 5.1,

[1]For an extended discussion of correcting split half estimates of reliability, see Salvia and Ysseldyke (1998).

Table 5.1. Split half reliability estimates for TABS scores, by group

Test	Obtained estimate	Corrected estimate
Children not at risk (n = 621)		
Detached	0.53	0.69
Hyper-sensitive/active	0.63	0.77
Underreactive	0.53	0.69
Dysregulated	0.49	0.66
TRI	0.72	0.84
Children with disabilities (n = 212)		
Detached	0.83	0.91
Hyper-sensitive/active	0.86	0.92
Underreactive	0.77	0.87
Dysregulated	0.68	0.81
TRI	0.91	0.95
Pooled sample (N = 833)		
Detached	0.84	0.91
Hyper-sensitive/active	0.81	0.90
Underreactive	0.76	0.86
Dysregulated	0.64	0.79
TRI	0.91	0.95

correcting the obtained correlations increases the estimates of reliability. In addition, as is apparent from the coefficients in Table 5.1, subtest reliabilities are substantially lower than the reliability of the total score. This finding is common and must be expected because the total obviously contains more items than any subtest.

Reliability is also affected by the range of scores of the children in the sample. Less variable samples produce lower estimates of reliability.[2] As shown in Table 5.2, means and standard deviations for children with disabilities were substantially higher for each subtest and *TRI*. Appropriate statistical analyses were used to compare the means of the children with disabilities with the children not believed to be at risk on each subtest and *TRI*; the analyses indicated that the means were different beyond a probability of .001. In addition, Bartlett's test comparing the variances of the children with disabilities with the children not believed to be at risk on each subtest and *TRI* were also significant beyond the .001 level. Because the group with disabilities was significantly more variable, we would expect the estimates of reliability to be higher for this group. The findings support this expectation.

For the three sample groups, the corrected TABS reliability is quite high (.88 for the children not at risk; .95 for the children with disabilities and for the pooled samples). This finding indicates that the *TRI* and the scores for *Detached* and *Hyper-sensitive/active* are sufficiently reliable to make important decisions on behalf of individual children. Reliabilities for *Underreactive* and *Dysregulated* are too low for individual decision making.

[2]For a discussion of the effect of constriction of range on a test's estimated reliability, see Salvia and Ysseldyke (1998).

Table 5.2. Means and standard deviations for TABS scores, by group

Test	*M*	*SD*
Children not at risk (*n* = 621)		
Detached	0.63	1.26
Hyper-sensitive/active	1.62	2.13
Underreactive	0.35	0.85
Dysregulated	0.35	0.79
TRI	2.95	3.40
Children with disabilities (*n* = 212)		
Detached	5.02	4.69
Hyper-sensitive/active	5.37	4.83
Underreactive	2.16	2.67
Dysregulated	1.29	1.64
TRI	13.84	9.85
Pooled sample (*N* = 833)		
Detached	1.75	3.23
Hyper-sensitive/active	2.58	3.46
Underreactive	0.81	1.72
Dysregulated	0.59	1.15
TRI	5.72	7.47

STANDARD ERRORS OF MEASUREMENT

The standard error of measurement (*SEM*) is a statistic that describes the variability of obtained scores around an individual's true score. In this case, an individual's true score is best thought of as the arithmetic average (mean) of possible subtests measuring the same ability with the same number of items. Standard errors of measurement are thought to be more variable for extreme scores than for scores near the mean. Rather than compute separate standard errors of measurement for each possible true score, an average standard error of measurement is estimated using the formula below, where *SD* is the standard deviation of the test and r_{xx} is the test's estimated reliability. Thus, the standard error of measurement is expressed in the same unit of measurement as the standard deviation of the test or subtest.

$$SEM = SD\sqrt{1 - r_{xx}}$$

Using the data in Tables 5.1 and 5.2, standard errors of measurement were estimated for each subtest and each group of children, both for raw scores and for standard scores.[3] These statistics appear in Table 5.3. Even though the standard deviations are generally larger in the sample of children with disabilities and the pooled sample, the standard errors of measurement are lower for these samples because the scores are more reliable.

[3]Subtest standard scores have a mean of 50 and a standard deviation of 10; *TRI* standard scores have a mean of 100 and a standard deviation of 15.

Table 5.3. Standard errors of measurement for TABS scores, by group

Test	Raw score *SEM*	Standard score *SEM*
Children not at risk (n = 621)		
Detached	0.69	5.50 (*SD* = 10)
Hyper-sensitive/active	0.85	3.98 (*SD* = 10)
Underreactive	0.47	5.47 (*SD* = 10)
Dysregulated	0.45	5.75 (*SD* = 10)
TRI	1.20	5.19 (*SD* = 15)
Children with disabilities (n = 212)		
Detached	1.49	3.07 (*SD* = 10)
Hyper-sensitive/active	1.34	2.79 (*SD* = 10)
Underreactive	1.00	3.57 (*SD* = 10)
Dysregulated	0.72	4.39 (*SD* = 10)
TRI	2.25	2.22 (*SD* = 15)
Pooled sample (N = 833)		
Detached	0.97	3.00 (*SD* = 10)
Hyper-sensitive/active	1.07	3.09 (*SD* = 10)
Underreactive	0.64	3.75 (*SD* = 10)
Dysregulated	0.55	4.76 (*SD* = 10)
TRI	1.62	2.17 (*SD* = 15)

STABILITY

Welteroth (1998) estimated the stability of TABS scores with a sample of 157 children who were reevaluated 2–3 weeks after their initial TABS Assessment Tools were completed. Overall, 97 children were diagnosed as not having disabilities, and 60 children were diagnosed as having disabilities. Most of these children (143) came from early intervention programs in central Pennsylvania. Children between 12 and 36 months received home-based programs, and children between 36 and 60 months attended preschool centers.

Because TABS scores are essentially not correlated with chronological age, stability was estimated across ages. As shown in Table 5.4, the stability coefficients for *TRI* and *Hyper-sensitive/active* scores exceed .90 for all samples; *Detached* scores exceed .90 for the sample with disabilities as well as the pooled sample. These coefficients indicate excellent stability. The remaining coefficients are generally in the .80s and acceptable for screening and research purposes.

There was a very consistent tendency for *TRI* and subtest scores to *decrease* between the test and the retest. These decreases were small, and the only difference that was statistically significant was for the *TRI*. We can hypothesize two reasons for the decreases. First, all of the children were receiving some educational services, and many of the children with disabilities were receiving a number of related services. These interventions may have had an effect on the *TRI*. Second, the decreases might be explained by extreme scores regressing. Further research is needed to clarify possible interpretations.

Table 5.4. Stability of TABS scores, by group

Test	r	Test M	Test SD	Retest M	Retest SD	Probability of difference
Children not at risk (n = 97)						
Detached	0.73	0.83	1.40	0.70	1.33	0.19
Hyper-sensitive/active	0.92	2.08	2.99	2.12	3.09	0.75
Underreactive	0.80	0.46	1.18	0.46	1.19	1.00
Dysregulated	0.73	0.44	0.96	0.38	0.81	0.36
TRI	0.91	3.81	5.02	3.66	5.25	0.50
Children with disabilities (n = 60)						
Detached	0.91	4.47	4.00	4.32	4.00	0.49
Hyper-sensitive/active	0.91	4.45	4.46	4.20	3.99	0.29
Underreactive	0.78	1.85	2.25	1.48	1.96	0.05
Dysregulated	0.88	1.12	1.72	1.02	1.61	0.36
TRI	0.93	11.88	8.56	11.02	8.20	0.04
Pooled sample (N = 157)						
Detached	0.92	2.22	3.23	2.08	3.20	0.17
Hyper-sensitive/active	0.92	2.98	3.79	2.90	3.59	0.56
Underreactive	0.81	0.99	1.80	0.85	1.60	0.10
Dysregulated	0.84	0.69	1.34	0.62	1.22	0.19
TRI	0.94	6.87	7.67	6.45	7.44	0.04

Reliability of Differences Between TABS Subtest Scores

We do not recommend using TABS subtest profiles for more precise diagnoses, because only some of the subtests have sufficient reliability for this purpose. Nonetheless, some clinicians and researchers may be interested in subtest differences; therefore, information about the reliability of the difference between any two subtests may be of use. However, we caution TABS users that just because a difference is reliable does not suggest that it is either rare or meaningful (Salvia & Good, 1982).

The reliability of the difference between two subtests is a function of the reliability of the specific subtests and their regression, weights, and intercorrelation.[4] When one subtest can be identified as the predictor and the other subtest can be identified as the predicted, then the procedure for estimating reliability recommended by Thorndike (1963) is preferred because it takes into account regression effects; however, in the absence of clearly identified independent and dependent variables, we prefer to estimate the reliability of the observed difference using the procedure recommended by Stake and Wardrop (1971). The reliability of the difference (rel_{dif}) can be estimated using the formula below, where r_{aa} is the reliability of one subtest, r_{bb} is the reliability of the other subtest, and r_{ab} is the correlation between the two subtests:

$$rel_{dif} = \frac{0.5(r_{aa} + r_{bb}) - r_{ab}}{1 - r_{ab}}.$$

[4]Differences in normative samples may also increase or attenuate observed differences; however, subtests normed on the same sample (e.g., TABS) do not have this problem.

Table 5.5. Intercorrelations among TABS subtests, by group

Test	Detached	Hyper-sensitive/ active	Underreactive
Children not at risk (n = 621)			
Hyper-sensitive/active	0.28		
Underreactive	0.40	0.12	
Dysregulated	0.17	0.26	0.10
Children with disabilities (n = 212)			
Hyper-sensitive/active	0.34		
Underreactive	0.48	0.02[a]	
Dysregulated	0.31	0.52	0.09[a]
Pooled sample (N = 833)			
Hyper-sensitive/active	0.51		
Underreactive	0.60	0.25	
Dysregulated	0.41	0.52	0.24

Note: Unless otherwise indicated, individual correlations are significant at .01.
[a]Not significant at .05.

The correlations between subtests for children not at risk, children with disabilities, and the pooled sample are found in Table 5.5. With two exceptions (*Underreactive* with *Hyper-sensitive/active* and *Dysregulated* with *Underreactive* for children with disabilities), all correlations in the pooled sample are significantly different from 0. The corrected split half coefficients (from Table 5.1) were used to calculate the reliability of subtest differences. These reliabilities are found in Table 5.6.

The standard error of measurement of an obtained difference is computed by using the usual formula; however, the standard deviation of an obtained difference must be calculated either from the actual differences or by using the formula shown below.

$$SD_{\mathrm{dif}} = \sqrt{SD_{\mathrm{a}}^2 + SD_{\mathrm{b}}^2 - 2r_{\mathrm{ab}}SD_{\mathrm{a}}SD_{\mathrm{b}}}.$$

Table 5.6. Reliability of obtained differences among TABS scores, by groups

Test	Detached	Hyper-sensitive/ active	Underreactive
Children not at risk (n = 621)			
Hyper-sensitive/active	0.62		
Underreactive	0.48	0.69	
Dysregulated	0.61	0.61	0.64
Children with disabilities (n = 212)			
Hyper-sensitive/active	0.87		
Underreactive	0.79	0.89	
Dysregulated	0.80	0.72	0.82
Pooled sample (N = 833)			
Hyper-sensitive/active	0.73		
Underreactive	0.62	0.84	
Dysregulated	0.69	0.68	0.77

The standard deviations for each sample and the pooled sample found in Table 5.2 and the intercorrelations found in Table 5.5 were used to calculate the standard deviations of the obtained differences (see Table 5.7).

Internal Consistency of the TABS Screener

Coefficient alpha (Cronbach, 1951) was used to estimate the internal consistency of the TABS Screener. Using the formula shown below (where k is the number of TABS Screener items and S^2 is the symbol for variance), alpha was found to be .83, a magnitude quite adequate for screening purposes. Using the variance of the pooled sample (7.154), the standard error of measurement of the TABS Screener is 1.10.

$$\text{alpha} = [k/(k-1)]\,[1 - (\Sigma S^2_{\text{items}}/S^2_{\text{test}})]$$

VALIDITY

Validity refers to the "appropriateness, meaningfulness, and usefulness of the specific inferences" one draws from a child's test performance (American Educational Research Association [AERA], 1985, p. 9). We intend two types of inference to be drawn from TABS ratings: 1) inferences about the presence of temperament and regulatory problems in young children and 2) inferences about the degree of such problems, if they are found. The first type of inference closely parallels what is commonly called *content validity,* or the extent to which TABS items are proper indicators of temperament and regulatory problems. The second type of inference closely parallels what is commonly called *construct validity,* or the extent to which TABS scores conform to hypotheses derived from the theory on which TABS was developed.

Does TABS Assess Temperament and Regulatory Problems?

Support for the content validity of TABS comes from two sources. First, the individual items were developed from extensive reviews of the theoretical

Table 5.7. Raw score (and standard score) standard errors of measurement of obtained differences among TABS scores, by groups

Test	Detached	Hyper-sensitive/active	Underreactive
Children not at risk (n = 621)			
Hyper-sensitive/active	2.15 (12.00)		
Underreactive	1.21 (10.95)	2.20 (13.27)	
Dysregulated	1.37 (12.88)	2.07 (12.17)	1.10 (13.42)
Children with disabilities (n = 212)			
Hyper-sensitive/active	5.47 (14.14)		
Underreactive	4.14 (14.00)	5.47 (14.00)	
Dysregulated	4.46 (11.75)	4.22 (9.80)	3.01 (13.49)
Pooled sample (N = 833)			
Hyper-sensitive/active	3.32 (14.14)		
Underreactive	2.59 (12.25)	3.46 (12.25)	
Dysregulated	2.95 (10.86)	3.03 (9.80)	1.83 (12.33)

and descriptive literature on various disorders of infancy and early childhood. The behaviors characteristically associated with these disorders became TABS items. Thus, the items that compose TABS are either characteristic of or highly associated with a variety of serious disorders of infancy and early childhood.

Second, four theoretically meaningful factors underlie TABS. The statistical methods and findings for establishing these factors have been provided in detail in the sections describing the development of TABS. Here we repeat that all four factors have Eigenvalues greater than 1 and that each factor accounts for at least 5% of the rotated variance. Most compelling, however, is that the factor structure of TABS is the same as that theorized independently by ZERO TO THREE: National Center for Infants, Toddlers, and Families in 1994.

Given the thoroughness of item development and item selection, we believe that TABS does assess temperament and regulatory problems in young children.

Do TABS Scores Act as One Would Expect?

Examination of TABS raw scores indicate that the subtest and total scores act as expected. First, given the nature of the behavior sampled, one should expect highly skewed distributions. Most children should earn scores of 0 or 1, with few children earning high scores. Indeed, in the sample of children who have not been identified as having disabilities, the distributions of TABS *TRI* scores and subtest scores are highly skewed.

Second, we would expect no relationship between TABS scores and chronological age. The behaviors sampled by TABS are not developmental; they are aberrant. We would not expect children to mature out of these behavior problems, although the problems can be treated with intervention. TABS scores are indeed unrelated to age. For that reason, separate norm tables are not provided for children of different ages.

Third, we would not expect a relationship between sex and aberrant behavior in children without disabilities. We found no differences in TABS scores between boys and girls without disabilities; however, we would expect to find sex differences within the population with disabilities because boys are diagnosed as having disabilities with much greater frequency than girls (U.S. Department of Education, 1992). We did find sex differences when the sex of the child was reported. We found that there were more boys than girls identified as having disabilities for every age group except 1-year-olds. Moreover, we found the TABS scores of boys were significantly ($p < .005$) higher (i.e., more deviant) than those of girls for *TRI*, *Detached*, and *Hypersensitive/active*; boys' scores were higher (but not significantly [$p < .05$]) than girls' scores for *Underreactive* or *Dysregulated*.

Fourth, because TABS behaviors are aberrant, we would expect children with disabilities to earn much higher scores on TABS than children who have not been identified as having disabilities. Indeed, children with disabilities do earn significantly and meaningfully greater scores on TABS than do children without disabilities. No children without disabilities receive *TRI* scores that equal or exceed the mean of the children with disabilities. On the TABS subtests, 3%–7% of the children not classified as having disabilities earn scores that equal or exceed the mean of children with disabilities.

Fifth, in a study of 42 children, we found that the aberrant behavior assessed by TABS generalizes across contexts. That sample contained 12 girls and 24 boys (sex data were not available for 6 children); 16 of the children were not identified as having disabilities, and 26 children were classified as having disabilities. The mean age of the children was 44.5 months (standard deviation = 14.5 months). The raters observed the children in different contexts. Parents observed their children in all of the usual nonschool environments: home, neighborhood, family gatherings, and so forth. Teachers or clinicians observed the children in more constrained environments: school, clinic, or assessment settings.[5] The raters each completed a TABS protocol, usually on the same day. TABS and factor scores were correlated. As shown in Table 5.8, the evaluations of the raters were moderately correlated. This finding suggests that the behaviors are exhibited across contexts.[6]

IS THE CATEGORIZATION OF TABS SCORES CORRECT?

As with any test, the interpretation of derived scores (i.e., percentiles and standard scores) is straightforward and seldom problematic; however, the categorization of scores is seldom validated. For example, many tests of intelligence and achievement presume that a score that is 2 or more standard deviations from the mean is an exception—exceptionally high or gifted, exceptionally low or delayed; yet there is very little evidence to support these categorizations.

We categorized *TRI*s into three levels. The first level identifies scores that do not demonstrate temperament and regulatory problems. Children who are not at risk earn *TRI*s less than 5. We believe this is a logical cutoff score because a larger percentage of children without disabilities earn these scores than do children identified as having disabilities. Children are considered at risk when they earn a *TRI* of 5 or more. We believe this is a logical cutoff score because the percentage of children with disabilities earning these scores is equal to or greater than the percentage of children not iden-

Table 5.8. Cross-context correlations for TABS scores

Test	*r*	*M*	*SD*
TABS	.64	11.6	10.4
Detached	.62	4.4	5.0
Hyper-sensitive/active	.42	4.2	4.4
Underreactive	.54	1.9	2.9
Dysregulated	.60	1.1	1.8

[5]These data should not be considered an indication of interrater reliability, because the behavior is not being observed simultaneously by the raters. It is better considered validity data. See Suen, Logan, Neisworth, and Bagnato (1995).

[6]Special thanks to Phoebe Rinkel, Valley Park Elementary School, Overland Park, Kansas, for providing interrater as well as stability data.

tified as having disabilities who earn these scores. Finally, we consider children to have temperament and regulatory disabilities when their *TRI* equals or exceeds 10. About 7% of the nonidentified population earn a score of 10, and about 4% receive scores of 11 or greater. However, more than 60% of the children with disabilities receive scores of 10. Thus, a score of 10 is infrequently associated with children without disabilities, whereas that score is usually associated with children with disabilities.

A Final Caution About TABS and Validity

The validity of an instrument and the inferences that can be based on an instrument are never established. Rather, one accepts the validity of an instrument when it has not been shown to be invalid. We have assessed TABS in what we believe to be the major areas that would indicate a lack of validity. We have found nothing to suggest that TABS is not valid. Future research can only add to our knowledge. We urge TABS users to send us the results of any research they might conduct with this scale.

Validity of the TABS Screener

The purpose of the TABS Screener is to identify children who are likely to be at risk or to have disabilities and who, therefore, should be assessed with the full TABS Assessment Tool. Thus, the only validity in which we are interested is the accuracy of the Screener in identifying children who do and children who do not require further evaluation, which is illustrated in Figure 5.1. When a child is predicted by the TABS Screener not to be at risk and is identified by the full Assessment Tool as not at risk, the prediction is correct. Similarly, when a child is predicted to be at risk (or to have a disability) by the Screener and is identified as being at risk (or having a disability) by the Assessment Tool, the prediction is accurate. However, when a child is predicted not to be at risk by the Screener and is identified by the Assessment Tool as being at risk (or as having a disability), the prediction is incorrect; that child is called a *false negative.* For screening devices, false negatives are the most serious type of error because those children do not receive follow-up evaluation. If a child is predicted to be at risk (or to have a disability) but is actually not at risk, the prediction is again inaccurate; this child is called a *false positive.* For screening devices, false positives decrease

		TABS SCREENER	
		Not at risk	**At risk**
TABS ASSESSMENT TOOL	**Not at risk**	accurate	*false positive*
	At risk	*false negative*	accurate

Figure 5.1. Screening accuracy, false negatives, and false positives.

<table>
<tr><td colspan="2" rowspan="2"></td><th colspan="2">TABS SCREENER</th></tr>
<tr><th>Not at risk</th><th>At risk</th></tr>
<tr><th rowspan="2">TABS ASSESSMENT TOOL</th><th>Not at risk</th><td>46.8% (n = 390)</td><td>14.5% (n = 121)</td></tr>
<tr><th>At risk</th><td>2.4% (n = 20)</td><td>36.3% (n = 302)</td></tr>
</table>

Figure 5.2. Accuracy of the TABS Screener.

efficiency because children who do not really require a follow-up evaluation (because they are not at risk or do not have a disability) receive one.

To evaluate the ability of the Screener to identify children in need of further assessment, we cross-tabulated the number of students in the pooled sample of 833 children with and without disabilities with TABS Screener scores of 1 or higher. This TABS Screener score actually predicts a *TRI* of 4, a score that was likely to increase the number of false positives. Given the prediction equation, however, a raw score of 2 predicts a *TRI* of 6, a score that would increase the number of false negatives. These cross-tabulations appear in Figure 5.2. As shown in that figure, most of the children (83%) are correctly classified by the TABS Screener. Of the 17% who are incorrectly classified, only 2.4% are false negatives, and these are all children who are at risk rather than with disabilities. About 14.5% of the incorrectly classified children are false positives, and only 6% of these children have disabilities. Thus, about 72% of the children who are screened as possibly at risk (or as having disabilities) will have been screened accurately.

6

Intervention

Guidelines for an Ecological Approach

Atypical behaviors in an infant or young child with special needs may serve as markers for more complex diagnoses (Neisworth, Bagnato, & Salvia, 1995), but the pinpointing of behaviors of concern may also be a first step in helping to normalize aspects of child development and family functioning that are affected by some of these atypical behaviors. Fortunately, there are actions that professionals can take to help children and families cope with challenging behavior. This chapter includes a rationale for providing early intervention for challenging behavior, followed by a description of a demonstration program aimed at providing specialized behavioral consultation services to families and early intervention personnel in a community-based early intervention program. The demonstration program used research editions of TABS to 1) document the need for such services within the program, 2) identify families in need of behavioral consultation, 3) pinpoint behaviors of concern for referred families, and 4) measure outcomes to document the effects of behavioral intervention. A case study involving sleep problems in an 11-month-old with multiple medical problems illustrates how TABS can be used in such a program.

NEED FOR EARLY INTERVENTION

Although many "typical" young children exhibit transitory behavior problems, there is mounting evidence that, for children with special needs, there is an increased risk for severe and persistent problems throughout their childhoods. The persistence of behavior problems can be one of the greatest obstacles to the healthy adjustment of children with special needs. Behavior problems can severely stress the parent–child relationship and other relationships in the immediate and extended family and are associated with coercive parenting styles that may, over time, exacerbate behavior difficulties and lead to an increased probability of abuse. Behavior problems can impede progress in educational and therapy programs. As problems become more difficult to manage, the risks to the child and the costs of providing intervention become more significant. As behaviors worsen, the likelihood that progressively more restrictive interventions will be used increases, posing additional risks that are often associated with those interventions. The presence of serious behavior problems in school-age children and young adults with special needs has been reported to be a significant factor in decisions to seek placements in more restrictive educational and residential environments and is reported to be a major cause of failed attempts at deinstitutionalization. Again, we see that significant aberrant behavior, either by itself or in addition to delayed development, must be considered as a serious developmental issue. Many specific methods are available for particular problems (e.g., bed-wetting). Although sometimes a "quick fix" for a specific problem is what should be done, many problems must be seen in context. The illustration and discussion that follow make clear that the approach taken is an ecological or systems approach, as opposed to a piecemeal, problem-specific focus.

A MODEL FOR COMMUNITY-BASED, FAMILY-CENTERED EARLY INTERVENTION

The Anne Arundel County (Maryland) Infants and Toddlers Program is a comprehensive, community-based program serving each year more than 300 families with children from birth to 36 months of age who have special needs. Through a state incentive grant process, this local program successfully piloted a model for providing behavioral consultation services to families of children with challenging behavior. To establish the need for such a service, staff and parents were surveyed using a preliminary version of TABS. Service coordinators completed the TABS Assessment Tool for 241 children enrolled in the program and indicated *Need Help* for at least one TABS item in 45% of those cases. When *parents* of new referrals were screened, 70% (n = 161) reported that they needed assistance with one or more TABS items.

With the need for service firmly established, a service delivery model was designed with input from parents and program staff. A behavioral specialist was contracted for 15–20 hours per week to provide varying levels of service to staff and families: staff consultation and training; brief consultation (one to three meetings) with parents; and short-term, intensive parent training and intervention. Parents and other early intervention team members could readily consult with a behavioral specialist soon after any member of the team raised questions regarding a behavior pattern of concern. The specialist consulted with the child's team to help them in varying degrees, depending on the specifics of the case. In those cases requiring more than parent information or support, the behavioral consultant would, in collaboration with team members, formulate a plan to assess the behaviors of concern and the factors that could be influencing the behaviors; offer guidance in developing intervention goals and strategies; provide training and feedback in intervention strategies; provide ongoing support to those implementing the plan; assist in evaluating and fine-tuning the program; plan for maintenance and generalization; and, if needed and when appropriate, make referrals to specialists at nearby pediatric teaching hospitals.

To identify candidates for the service, a brief behavior checklist was added to the intake questionnaire (the TABS Screener was not available at that time). If any concerns regarding behavior were expressed, the parent was asked to complete the full TABS Assessment Tool. When the need for assistance was indicated, the service coordinator and the parents met to share additional information about the behavior (e.g., detailed descriptions of the behavior, when it occurred, strategies used by the parents, risks to the child, any other information the parents thought relevant), discuss options such as additional information for parents or staff (e.g., readings, instructional videotapes, workshops), additional support (e.g., from family, other parents, staff), and behavioral consultation service (e.g., for additional information, support, help in designing an assessment or intervention, referral to another specialist).

A behavior-reduction decision model (Wolery, Bailey, & Sugai, 1988) provided a framework for assessment and intervention in those cases requiring more than information and support. (See Wolery & Fleming, 1993, for an excellent review of goals, assumptions and decision models for coping with problem behavior.) The behavioral consultant led the team through each of the following steps:

1) Identify the Problem and Restate it as a Goal

The purpose of this step is to determine whether a problem exists and to identify its type. The completed TABS Assessment Tool serves as a starting point for pinpointing the problem behavior. Based on TABS results, interviews provide precise and detailed descriptions of the problem, including specific behaviors exhibited by the child, estimates of frequencies, durations, intensities, and conditions under which the problem does and does not occur. Parents and staff are encouraged to describe the desired outcome.

2) Assess Behavior, Function, and Risk/Protective Factors

This vital step focuses on whether the behavior is a function, in part, of age, developmental level, medical condition, parenting factors, or the parent–child relationship; and whether the behavior warrants intervention efforts. Because behavior is lawful but controlled and influenced by multiple factors, it is crucial to identify those factors that may be related to the problem. At this step, an attempt is made to determine whether a child's basic needs are being met, the functions(s) of the problem behavior, whether and why the child uses the problem behavior instead of more adaptive and socially acceptable responses, and whether the behavior is somehow being inadvertently reinforced.

Many factors influence behavior and resiliency in a young child with special needs. To develop an effective, realistic, and individualized plan for addressing family concerns regarding problem behaviors, it is important to identify risk and protective factors. We refer to these as *child, parent, environmental,* and *relationship factors. Child factors* include constitutional (e.g., health status, temperament, sensory abilities, regulatory factors) and developmental (e.g., strengths and weaknesses in communication; cognition; social, emotional, and motor abilities) factors. *Parent factors* include parental age, health status, parenting style, psychiatric and psychological factors (e.g., depression, resolution of diagnostic status), knowledge and skills related to child rearing and discipline, parental expectations, availability of and skill in using support networks, and culture.

When we consider *environmental factors,* we ask whether the child's basic physical needs (food, clothing, shelter, medical intervention) are being met, whether the amount and variety of stimulation are adequate, whether a daily schedule and basic routines are followed, and whether the environment is predictable and hazard-free. *Relationship factors* include parent–child attachment, number of different caregivers, and quality of parent–child interactions in a variety of situations. The behavioral consultant asks the staff member to describe risk and protective factors in each of the four areas, as well as possible payoffs for the behavior (e.g., the child engages in the behavior to get something, to avoid something, to communicate a want or a need, because it feels good).

3) Specify an Objective for the Intervention

If the behavior poses a medical or safety risk to the child or to others, significantly impairs family functioning, interferes with educational or therapeutic activities, or poses a significant risk to materials or equipment, then some type of immediate intervention is warranted. At this step the parent and consulting team members describe in writing the anticipated outcome and modify the IFSP to include this objective.

Usually, the objective is stated to reflect a desired change in child behavior (e.g., decrease the number of aggression episodes per week from 15 to 5). In some cases, however, after considering all the information gathered in Step 2, the team determines that it is not appropriate to directly modify the child's behavior. In these situations, the focus is on reducing risk factors and increasing protective factors. The objective may then reflect a desired change in the environment or in a parent behavior (e.g., the child will have an outing at least once each day, the child's number of naps per day will be reduced from two to one).

4) Collect Baseline Data on the Problem Behavior

A variety of techniques can be used to establish baselines of problem behaviors (Cooper, Heron, & Heward, 1987). In an early intervention program, parents are likely to be responsible for this task, which can be quite a challenge if staff fail to communicate the importance of the intervention and recommend a technique that is practical. We encourage parents to make periodic home videotapes of their problem situations. Baseline videotapes aid in defining the target behavior and assessing parent response to the behavior; they can easily be viewed with the parents and used as an instructional tool; and they provide a powerful contrast when paired with postintervention videotapes.

5) Plan the Intervention

This step is a two-phase education process which is led by the behavioral specialist and involves all team members. In the first phase, information from the previous steps is reviewed, and intervention options, derived from the research literature, are described. Pros and cons of each option are reviewed, and the parents choose or, with assistance from the rest of the team, develop a plan that best fits with their interpretation of the assessment information and the style, needs, and resources of the family.

In the second and equally important phase, team members who will be involved in implementing the intervention are trained. Correct procedures are demonstrated and often videotaped for later reference. Every member of the team practices the procedures and is given feedback. Written recommendations are also provided, and team members are encouraged to anticipate problems that may arise and agree in advance on how to address those challenges.

In cases in which the plan involves linking the family to resources that can help modify risk and protective factors (e.g., mother decides to seek help for depression), the steps involved in that process are reviewed and team assistance is offered as needed.

6) Implement the Intervention and Ensure Correct Implementation

When intervention involves changing antecedents or consequences for target behaviors, modifying schedules or routines, or providing opportunities to strengthen alternative behaviors, parents are typically the agents for change. To ensure correct implementation, program staff maintain frequent contact to assist with troubleshooting and to provide much-needed encouragement. The first few days of intervention are viewed as a learning situation for the parents, who need feedback as they master the intervention strategies. The frequency of home visits is increased, and if parents encounter a crisis, an on-call staff member is available for assistance, at least by telephone. In those cases in which intervention involves linking the family to resources (e.g., counseling, respite care), staff are encouraged to probe for compliance, and, when parents report obstacles, staff are encouraged to help parents generate strategies for overcoming those obstacles.

7) Monitor Progress and Implementation

The behavioral consultant is updated every 7–14 days once there is evidence that the intervention is being implemented correctly and that the parent will request help if it is needed. Updates can be through contact with the referring staff member, telephone contact with the parents, or a home visit, depending on the case. Programs are modified and fine-tuned as needed.

8) Evaluate Progress

A schedule for evaluating progress is developed when the IFSP is modified to include the objective(s) addressing the problem behavior(s). The evaluation typically involves review of data, videotapes, and parent reports.

ILLUSTRATION OF AN INTERVENTION PROGRAM

Amy was an 11-month-old infant with multiple diagnoses including prematurity, athetoid cerebral palsy, possible visual problems (neurologically based), and global developmental delay. Her mother had been referred to ZERO TO THREE: National Center for Infants, Toddlers, and Families when

Amy was 7 months old. An IFSP included service coordination, transportation, home- and center-based parent training, infant stimulation, occupational therapy, and physical therapy. General recommendations regarding sleep problems were provided by the service coordinator.

When Amy was 9 months old, a referral was made for behavioral consultation services. Staff requested more specific readings related to sleep problems and suggestions for providing Amy's 18-year-old mother with more support. The sleep problems failed to improve after 2 additional months. Amy's mother reported that the sleep problems were significantly disrupting her ability to participate in early intervention activities and disrupting her partner's sleep and work schedule. She reported that she felt she was at risk for abusing Amy because of her own severe sleep deprivation.

1) Identify the Problem and Restate it as a Goal

Amy's mother reported that Amy had always cried intensely and for long periods when she was put to bed; that she rarely fell asleep on her own; and that when she did sleep, it was for short periods (less than 2 hours). She stated that her highest priority for Amy was establishing a sleep schedule. Her goal was to get Amy to sleep through the night and take regular naps during the day.

2) Assess Behavior, Function, and Risk/Protective Factors

The team considered several questions before beginning the assessment process. Exactly what kind of sleep problems was Amy experiencing? Were they related to her age, developmental level, medical condition, or parenting factors, or were they influenced by the parent–child relationship? How much sleep should she be getting, and why had she not established a better sleep routine? Were there any payoffs for Amy or her mother that might be encouraging the problem sleep patterns?

The behavioral specialist met with Amy's mother at her home and asked her to describe Amy's sleep patterns, how they evolved over time, and her insights into the problem. From her mother's description, it appeared that Amy was experiencing frequent waking, waking for feeding, difficulty getting to sleep, difficulty sleeping alone, and unusual sleep cycle (see Ferber, 1985; Huntley, 1991). She revealed that because her partner was working very long hours, she feared Amy's crying would disrupt his sleep schedule. She explained that she had read about parenting tips on how to encourage typical sleep patterns, but she encountered several problems. First, she was concerned that, because Amy had so many medical problems, she was uncomfortable letting her cry for extended periods. She feared crying would induce a seizure or heart problems. She also reported that sometimes Amy's intense, shrill crying made her so angry that she was afraid she would lose her temper and hurt her. She reported that she held Amy nearly continuously, partly to prevent Amy from crying and partly because it helped her to feel close to her child.

During this meeting, Amy's mother was encouraged to call her pediatrician and discuss her concerns regarding medical complications. She did so, and her pediatrician verified that Amy had no medical problems that would be exacerbated by crying and strongly encouraged her to work on establishing a more typical sleep routine. After about 2 hours of directed but supportive discussions, Amy's mother concluded that she was unwittingly encouraging Amy's problem behavior by constantly holding her and that there was more she could do to encourage her to learn to sleep on her own.

3) Specify an Objective for the Intervention

Amy's atypical sleep pattern clearly warranted intervention: It significantly disrupted family functioning and interfered with her therapy schedule. With guidance from parenting books and trusted mentors (including early intervention professionals), the objective was for Amy to develop typical bedtime and sleep patterns. Ideally, she would sleep from 9 P.M. to 7 A.M. and nap from 1 P.M. to 3 P.M.

4) Collect Baseline Data on the Problem Behavior

From the first consultation, Amy's mother was encouraged to keep a daily sleep log (including a description of activities preceding sleep, as well as sleep and wakening times, and a description of how she [Amy's mother] handled awakenings and crying). This log revealed that Amy was sleeping approximately 9–14 hours per 24-hour period, with night sleep duration from 6.5 to 9.25 hours in length, and was taking two to six naps per day, ranging from .25 to 2.5 hours in length. The log also revealed that Amy nearly always fell asleep in her mother's arms, awakened when her mother tried to transfer her to her own bed, and was immediately comforted by her mother when she fussed.

5) Plan the Intervention

The behavioral consultant, Amy's mother, and the service coordinator met to plan the intervention. After reviewing and discussing several books for parents on sleep problems, Amy's mother elected the intervention approach referred to by Huntley (1991) as the "cry it out approach." This approach assumes that the payoff for crying, which serves to reinforce the behavior, is parent attention. As the parent attempts to comfort the crying child, she interferes with the child's development of independent sleep habits. Intervention involves letting the child cry, possibly for extended periods, so that she can learn to put herself to sleep.

Parent training included development of a simple bedtime routine for Amy (bath, pajamas, crib, pacifier, blanket, lullaby tape, nightlight, consistent nap- and bedtime), and development of plans for the parents when Amy cried (distraction strategies included listening to a relaxation tape, reading, watching television with ear plugs if necessary, asking spouse for support, or contacting on-call team members for assistance).

6) Implement the Intervention and Ensure Correct Implementation

A target date was identified, and the specialist maintained daily contact during the first week to help clarify the procedures, troubleshoot, and offer encouragement. Several home visits were made to observe the bedtime routine and provide feedback. Sometimes Amy's crying was so intense that her mother gave in and picked her up. When she revealed these lapses in the protocol, she was encouraged to use the self-monitoring scale and reminded to contact a friend or the on-call staff member for suggestions and encouragement, which she began to do. She also occasionally suspended the protocol when she suspected that Amy was sick, and she was assured by the team that this was a reasonable option.

7) Monitor Progress and Implementation

Amy's mother used a checklist to record the implementation of the bedtime routine, and she noted the time Amy was put to bed and the time she stopped crying and fell asleep. In addition, she monitored her own reaction to Amy's crying using a five-point rating scale (1= I am comfortable ignoring her crying; 5 = I feel like I'm going to lose control of my actions, and I need to call someone for support). As she reported increased comfort with the program and as Amy's schedule gradually normalized, team members attenuated their monitoring contacts (telephone calls and home visits) from several times per day to weekly telephone calls and home visits.

8) Evaluate Progress

Amy's crying at bedtime decreased from 1–3 hours the first week to 15–55 minutes each time she was put to bed (for either nap- or bedtime) during the second week. Crying at bedtime continued, but the duration decreased gradually over the course of several months. The program was suspended several times when Amy developed ear infections, but each time her mother was able to restart the program. On several occasions, she reported that she considered stopping the program but chose instead to contact a support person (a friend or the on-call team member).

CONCLUSION

TABS has been helpful in documenting the need for behavioral services in community-based early intervention programs, identifying families that need help with the challenging behaviors of their young children, and pinpointing behaviors of concern. This chapter describes a model for providing community-based early intervention for behavior problems and illustrates how the behavior-reduction decision model can provide a framework for assessing complex behavior problems that require ecological or systems-based approaches.

7

Research-Based Specific Interventions

Many methods have been described in journal articles, research reports, and texts that are reported to be effective for specific problems with selected children. Although databased effectiveness is often demonstrated, collateral or subsequent data may not be reported. Furthermore, many interventions may not be feasible in contexts other than the ones involved in the studies. Frequently, the intervention is a suggested general strategy, such as using task analysis, manual prompting, planned ignoring, or an immediate reward. Most of the intervention suggestions in the literature are based on behavior principles. We rush to recognize, however, that other approaches (e.g., counseling, family social work, medical interventions) are sometimes approaches of choice. This chapter, then, should be viewed as a fraction of the intervention suggestions related to each item that might be described.

Within the fields of early intervention and developmental disabilities, research has been sparse on the classification and management of low-incidence challenging behaviors in infants and young children. Much research has focused on the management of high-incidence behaviors such as ADHD and oppositional and defiant behavior, perhaps as precursors to later conduct disorders. However, research on the incidence and management of infant and early childhood behaviors such as self-stimulation and self-injury, severe social withdrawal, hypersensitivities, and serious problems with arousal and sensory and physiological modulation has been sparse. It is clear that much future research must be directed to management of early extremes of temperament and self-regulation. In view of the dearth in this area, we include a selective review of some documented research studies; we recognize that this is an area requiring much greater study with practical implications for practitioners.

Although many of the cited strategies may be appropriate for a given behavior, others may seem too general and imprecise; nevertheless, this chapter offers a beginning link to the behaviors in the TABS Assessment Tool. The professional is advised to consider the specific interventions for possible use in a broader treatment plan, as described and illustrated in Chapter 6. Interventions described in the literature for each TABS item are organized under the four TABS factors. We especially emphasize the importance of positive behavioral support and nonaversive interventions.

DETACHED ITEMS

1 Consistently upset by changes in schedule

- Analyze transitions to determine where the problems lie. During transitions, make directions clear, repeat them if necessary, and provide immediate praise for compliance.
- Use a token system to make changes more pleasant. Break the steps of transitions into several parts, and give the child one point for each step followed correctly.
- Have distinct labels for each area of a home or school. Develop signals, such as ringing a bell or moving a character on a flannel board, to designate when children should make a transition. Reinforce going to the correct area and following the correct signal for transitions.

2 Emotions don't match what is going on

- If a child is giggling or laughing inappropriately, peers, parents, or caregivers should model appropriate responses. Reactions to the child's behavior should be consistent. Use reinforcement when the child is acting appropriately.
- When a child is displaying inappropriate social behaviors, redirect her focus and limit the amount of attention she receives. Praise the child for shaking hands or patting a friend on the back. Give intermittent rewards to the child during intervals when undesirable behaviors have not been displayed. Help the child to develop appropriate alternative behaviors on her own, and give the child ongoing feedback regarding her behaviors and progress.
- When a child is displaying extreme anger, his patterns of behavior should be analyzed. Triggers should be identified. Many times a child follows the same chain of behaviors prior to reaching peak anger. A description of which specific actions the child takes should be made.

3 Seems to look through or past people

- A child displaying this behavior should be checked for hearing difficulty and depression. A consultation with a psychologist might be considered.
- Ask the child to repeat short statements and explain what the statements mean while maintaining eye contact.
- Use a shaping procedure to teach the child to make eye contact. First, shape looking at you on cue, such as by saying, "Look at me." Later, reward child-initiated eye contact.

4 Resists looking you in the eye

- Ask the child to repeat short statements and explain what the statements mean.
- Use a shaping procedure to teach the child to make eye contact. First, shape looking at you on cue, such as by saying, "Look at me." Later, reward child-initiated eye contact.
- Combining *differential reinforcement of other* (DRO) plus *differential reinforcement of incompatible* (DRI) behaviors with an interruption program may be more effective than DRO plus DRI without interruption. Block the child's line of vision to interrupt his stare until he redirects his gaze, and give a verbal redirection such as, "Look at me."

5 Acts like others are not there

- A child displaying this behavior should be checked for hearing difficulty and depression. A consultation with a psychologist might be considered.
- Ask the child to repeat short statements and explain what the statements mean.

6 Hardly ever starts on own to play with others

- Pair two children who are already familiar with each other. Model sharing and joint play. Allow children to play, and praise them for joint play. If children are not playing together, use brief reminders.
- Take pictures of activity and peer choices. Allow the child to select an activity and playmates using the pictures. Model interactions, and praise the child's use of the pictures. Use successive approximations to teach increasing levels of associative play (i.e., play with other children involving sharing, borrowing, helping).
- Allow children time for free play, and encourage appropriate play by giving reinforcement. Correct children who are playing inappropriately.
- Do a task analysis of appropriate play, and use graduated guidance to teach behaviors. Teach behaviors three times per day, and interrupt inappropriate play.

7 Moods and wants are too hard to figure out

- Teach the child how to express her wants and needs in responsible ways. Teach the child how to use "I" messages to express her feelings. Use role-play, modeling, practice, and precorrections. Warn the child that she may not get her way. Explain how the child can act appropriately, and give ongoing feedback during practice and real situations. A reward-and-consequence system can be set up for appropriate and inappropriate expressive behaviors. When redirection is given, it should be subtle, and frequent attention should be given to the child for appropriate behavior.
- Teach the child to use a picture board to point to pictures portraying how he is feeling or what he wants.

- Parents may need to seek training in functional behavior to help them learn to discern which functions the behaviors serve.

8 Seems to be in "own world"

- A child displaying this behavior should be checked for hearing difficulty and depression. A consultation with a psychologist might be considered.
- Ask the child to repeat short statements and explain what the statements mean.

9 Often stares into space

- A child displaying this behavior should be checked for hearing difficulty and depression. A consultation with a psychologist might be considered.
- Ask the child to repeat short statements and explain what the statements mean.
- If the child seems to "tune out," he may be experiencing a seizure. If the child does have seizures, the appropriate intervention depends on the type of seizure. There are several types of seizures, and each type requires a different response. In the case of a small absence seizure, just repeat anything you have said and make sure the child hears you. For a simple partial seizure, comfort and reassure the child. A complex seizure requires that you remove dangerous objects, calmly take the child to a quiet place, and offer soothing reassurance. The most severe generalized tonic-clonic seizure requires that you protect the child from injury by placing a soft object under his head, turning the child on his side, waiting for consciousness, and letting the seizure run its course. If a child displays jerky movements, a helmet should be used. In all cases, you should describe to the child what seizures and epilepsy are. Discuss with the child how he feels, and do not overprotect him. Medication can be used to prevent seizures when taken on a regular schedule.

10 "Tunes out," loses contact with what is going on

- A child displaying this behavior should be checked for hearing difficulty and depression. A consultation with a psychologist might be considered.
- If the child seems to "tune out," he may be experiencing a seizure. If the child does have seizures, the appropriate intervention depends on the type of seizure. There are several types of seizures, and each type requires a different response. In the case of a small absence seizure, just repeat anything you have said and make sure the child hears you. For a simple partial seizure, comfort and reassure the child. A complex seizure requires that you remove dangerous objects, calmly take the child to a quiet place, and offer soothing reassurance. The most severe generalized tonic-clonic seizure requires that you protect the child from injury by placing a soft object under his head, turning the child on his side, waiting for consciousness, and letting the seizure run its course. If a child displays jerky movements, a helmet should be used. In all cases, you should

describe to the child what seizures and epilepsy are. Discuss with the child how he feels and do not overprotect him. Medication can be used to prevent seizures when taken on a regular schedule.

11 Plays with toys in strange ways

- Allow children time for free play, and encourage appropriate play by giving reinforcement. Correct children who are playing inappropriately.
- Remove toys, books, or other items when the child uses them inappropriately or strangely.
- Do a task analysis of appropriate play, and use graduated guidance to teach behaviors. Teach behaviors three times per day, and interrupt inappropriate play.
- Controlled use of music in combination with modeling over time has been used to shift a child's focus from her obsessive interest in an object to another object and eventually to another person.

12 Plays with toys as if confused by how they work

- Allow children time for free play, and encourage appropriate play by giving reinforcement. Correct children playing inappropriately.
- Do a task analysis of appropriate play, and use graduated guidance to teach behaviors. Teach behaviors three times per day, and interrupt inappropriate play.
- Use brief teaching sessions to teach the child how to maintain her attention. Praise the child for paying attention, and ask the child questions periodically.

13 Makes strange throat noises

- If the child has been diagnosed with Tourette syndrome, the child's physician must be consulted as to which behaviors the child is capable of controlling and changing. Focus on only one behavior at a time. Collect anecdotal information to determine which behavior to address initially.
- Utilize prompts (nonverbal, verbal), modeling (e.g., say, "Want drink?"), and praise to encourage the use of verbal language instead of strange noises. Providing interesting materials (some out of reach), presenting choices, acting in an absurd manner, and creating situations where the child will need assistance all help to increase verbal language.
- As with any unwanted behavior, take great care to avoid providing attention or other rewards contingent on the strange noises.

14 Disturbed by too much light, noise, or touching

- Through positive reinforcement of successive approximations, children have successfully overcome aversions to being touched, seeing bright lights, or hearing loud or unusual sounds. Positively reinforce when the child remains undisturbed when exposed to a small amount of light, noise, or touch. Gradually increase the amount of light, noise, or touch, reinforcing the desired behavior.

- *In vivo* systematic desensitization is especially effective for preschoolers, young children, or children with developmental delays that place them at age 7 years or younger. *In vivo* procedures do not involve asking children to imagine the situation; instead, actual circumstances are encountered. Again, proceeding gradually is the imperative. Someone who fears bridges, for example, should be encouraged to master very low, short bridges before moving on to greater challenges.
- Let the child know that you are available to talk. If a child is acting nervous, react consistently. Redirect the child to what he or she should be doing. Teach relaxation, identification of oncoming stress, and coping strategies. Some examples of strategies are counting backward and practicing muscle relaxation.
- A back massager or tape recorder can calm a child. Pair the reinforcing activity with another activity that is not as enjoyable for the child. Use the reinforcer only if the child is calmly participating in the less desirable activity. If the child cries, remove the massager or tape recorder. When the child stops crying, return the reinforcer.

15 Overexcited in crowded places

- Through positive reinforcement of successive approximations, children have successfully overcome aversions, including overreacting in the presence of crowds. Positively reinforce when the child remains relatively calm when in the presence of two people. Gradually increase the number of people until the child can tolerate larger groups and eventually crowds.
- Various behavioral techniques have been successfully used to reduce hypersensitivity and anxiety in children. In cognitive systematic desensitization, a child is asked to imagine each step of an individualized hierarchy while she engages in a response that is incompatible with the fear (e.g., eating a snack, playing with a desired toy, singing). For example, the child can imagine (or be shown pictures of) increasing numbers of people until small groups and then crowds no longer evoke overreaction. Children close to the child's age can model the appropriate behavior involving the fear stimulus, followed by guided practice and reinforcement of the appropriate behavior. Confrontation of the feared stimulus by the child is critical to effective treatment.
- *In vivo* systematic desensitization is especially effective for preschoolers, young children, or children with developmental delays that place them at age 7 years or younger. *In vivo* procedures do not involve asking children to imagine the situation; instead, actual circumstances are encountered. Again, proceeding gradually is the imperative. Someone who fears bridges, for example, should be encouraged to master very low, short bridges before moving on to greater challenges.
- Let the child know that you are available to talk. If a child is acting nervous, react consistently. Redirect the child to what he should be doing.

Teach relaxation, identification of oncoming stress, and coping strategies. Some examples of strategies are counting backward and practicing muscle relaxation.

- If a child has an exaggerated fear of a particular object or situation, *counterconditioning* and *extinction* should be used. Start to slowly expose the child to the fearful event in small steps. Using *vicarious* desensitization, have the child watch others touch a feared object or participate in a feared activity. *Contact* desensitization involves having an instructor or parent help the child touch an object or participate in an activity. Contact desensitization has been shown to result in less avoidance of the fearful item or activity. In all cases, allow successive approximations toward the actual item or event.

16 Stares at lights

- Because suppression of one form of self-stimulation may lead to an increase in another form, the child should be helped to develop a form that is more socially acceptable and less interfering with learning.
- Combining *differential reinforcement of other* (DRO) plus *differential reinforcement of incompatible* (DRI) behaviors with an interruption program may be more effective than DRO plus DRI without interruption. Block the child's line of vision to interrupt his stare until he redirects his gaze, and give a verbal redirection such as, "Look at me."
- Controlled use of music in combination with modeling over time has been used to shift a child's focus from obsessive interest in an object to another object and eventually to another person.

17 Overly interested in toy/object

- Controlled use of music in combination with modeling over time has been used to shift a child's focus from obsessive interest in an object to another object and eventually to another person.
- Fifteen minutes of continuous and vigorous exercise (e.g., jogging) as compared with mild exercise (e.g., ball playing) reduces subsequent stereotypic behaviors in young children.
- When given a soft toy (as compared with a hard toy or a toy with wheels), higher levels of self-stimulation have been demonstrated. Awareness of the effect that specific types of toys may have on children's stereotypic behaviors should guide the selection of toys for home and school.
- Because suppression of one form of self-stimulation may lead to an increase in another form, the child should be helped to develop a form that is more socially acceptable and less interfering with learning.
- Observing the kinds of self-stimulation that the child prefers and substituting an appropriate toy may result in substituting socially acceptable play for the self-stimulating behavior. For the replacement of vestibular stimulation (e.g., hand flapping), introduce toys and activities that are similar to the self-stimulating motion, such as bouncing a ball or hitting a tambourine.

18 Flaps hands over and over

- Encourage the child to sit on his hands or keep them in his pockets.
- Fifteen minutes of continuous and vigorous exercise (e.g., jogging) as compared with mild exercise (e.g., ball playing) reduces subsequent stereotypic behaviors in young children.
- When given a soft toy (as compared with a hard toy or a toy with wheels), higher levels of self-stimulation have been demonstrated. Awareness of the effect that specific types of toys may have on children's stereotypic behaviors should guide the selection of toys for home and school.
- Because suppression of one form of self-stimulation may lead to an increase in another form, the child should be helped to develop a form that is more socially acceptable and less interfering with learning.
- Observing the kinds of self-stimulation that the child prefers and substituting an appropriate toy may result in substituting socially acceptable play for the self-stimulating behavior. For the replacement of vestibular stimulation (e.g., hand flapping), introduce toys and activities that are similar to the self-stimulating motion, such as bouncing a ball or hitting a tambourine.
- Several behavioral interventions have been effective in eliminating rhythmic body movements, such as overpracticing an incompatible behavior (e.g., arm exercises), *differential reinforcement of other* (DRO) behaviors (e.g., appropriate play with a toy), reinforcement of nonoccurrence of the target behavior, mild punishment, and extinction.

19 Shakes head over and over

- Fifteen minutes of continuous and vigorous exercise (e.g., jogging) as compared with mild exercise (e.g., ball playing) reduces subsequent stereotypic behaviors in young children.
- Because suppression of one form of self-stimulation may lead to an increase in another form, the child should be helped to develop a form that is more socially acceptable and less interfering with learning.
- Use a *differential reinforcement of lower levels* program in which attention and other reinforcement are given for progressively lower rates of head shaking.

20 Wanders around without purpose

- A child displaying this behavior should be checked for depression. A consultation with a psychologist might be considered.
- Little attention should be given to the child when acting apathetically. Behavior that is appropriate for the situation should be reinforced.
- Structure a two- then three-step (and so forth) activity sequence with reinforcers for completing each activity. Provide immediate corrective feedback when child strays from activity or sequence.

Resources

Following is a list of resources that give more detailed information on intervention strategies related to *Detached* problems. Full citations can be found in the reference list at the end of the manual.

Baker (1982).
Bech (1993).
Bell (1986).
Blackman & Silberman (1971).
Blechman (1985).
Fellner, LaRoche, & Sulzer-Azaroff (1984).
Gersh (1991).
Kern, Koegel, & Dunlap (1984).
Lovaas (1981).
Lyman & Hembree-Kigin (1994).
Sprick & Howard (1995).
Watters & Wood (1983).

HYPER-SENSITIVE/ACTIVE ITEMS

21 Upset by every little thing

- A back massager or tape recorder can calm a child. Pair the reinforcing activity with another activity that is not as enjoyable for the child. Use the reinforcer only if the child is calmly participating in the less desirable activity. If the child cries, remove the massager or tape recorder. When the child stops crying, return the reinforcer.
- If a child is upset, explain that everyone is unhappy at times but that the feeling will go away. Explain options for coping with annoyances, such as thinking happy thoughts. When the child expresses unhappiness, wait a short while (so that this behavior is not unwittingly encouraged), have the child verbalize a happy thought, and then give the child praise and affection.

22 Often difficult to soothe when upset and crying

- An infant who is colicky will fuss, cry, and be irritable for 3 hours or more, at least 3 days a week. You must cope with the distress until the infant outgrows it. Movement, noises, and tactile stimulation in the form of car rides, putting the baby seat on a washing machine while it is running, or walking while holding the infant may help quiet the child.
- A back massager or tape recorder can calm a child. Pair the reinforcing activity with another activity that is not as enjoyable for the child. Use the reinforcer only if the child is calmly participating in the less desirable activity. If the child cries, remove the massager or tape recorder. When the child stops crying, return the reinforcer.
- Record the frequency of a child's crying or whining. Use *differential reinforcement of other behavior* (DRO) by giving points or tokens and

praise to the child for not crying or whining. Use *differential reinforcement of incompatible behavior* (DRI) by giving a sticker to the child each time he complies without any complaints.

23 Has wide swings in mood

- Repeated wide mood swings may be a sign of emotional disturbance. A psychological evaluation might be considered if mood swings are drastic and recurring; pharmacological intervention may be helpful.
- An infant who is colicky will fuss, cry, and be irritable for 3 hours or more, at least 3 days a week. You must cope with the distress until the infant outgrows it. Movement, noises, and tactile stimulation in the form of car rides, putting the baby seat on a washing machine while it is running, or walking while holding the infant may help quiet the child.

24 Gets angry too easily

- When a child is displaying extreme anger, his behavior should be analyzed. Triggers should be identified. Many times a child follows the same chain of behaviors prior to reaching peak anger. A description of which specific actions the child takes should be made.
- Once a description of the behavior is made, you and the child should identify self-control strategies to redirect the anger. Some examples include counting backward from 10, deep breathing, positive self-talk, self-imposed time-out, deep muscle relaxation, and using "I" messages to communicate how she feels. These strategies should be modeled and practiced, and feedback should be given to the child.
- If consequences for behaviors associated with anger are necessary, they should be logically tied to the behavior. Before allowing the child to return to activities, you should talk to him about what happened and how he could have handled things differently. All attempts the child makes to maintain self-control should be reinforced.
- Professional assistance might be necessary in cases of extreme anger. All other physical or neurological possibilities should be ruled out.

25 Too easily frustrated

- *Learned helplessness* refers to children learning that they can do nothing on their own. Social-skills training in independence and proper ways to ask for help should be taught. When responding to inappropriate behaviors, be consistent. Reinforce all attempts the child makes to self-help.
- Teach the child skills to be more self-reliant. Use *precorrections*—remind the child to ask herself if she really needs help before asking an adult.
- Certain self-control strategies may be helpful. Some examples include counting backward from 10, deep breathing, positive self-talk, self-imposed time-out, deep muscle relaxation, and using "I" messages to communicate how she feels. These strategies should be modeled and practiced, and feedback should be given to the child.

26 Has wild temper tantrums

- Time-out is recommended for many children showing extreme behavior. A room should be designated for time-out that closes but has no lock. The room should not have a television or any dangerous items. Leave books and toys in the room to give the child the opportunity to self-soothe. Time-out for children who may want to be alone (e.g., some children with autism) is not appropriate.
- As soon as the child begins to have a tantrum, put the child in time-out. Do not threaten; just say, "Time-out," and guide the child to the room immediately. Five minutes is the recommended time period for the child in time-out. If the child comes out of the room before the designated time, guide him back in, and reset the timer. Physical force should not be used unless absolutely necessary.
- Once a description of the behavior is made, you and the child should identify self-control strategies to replace the tantrums. Some examples include counting backward from 10, deep breathing, positive self-talk, self-imposed time-out, deep muscle relaxation, and using "I" messages to communicate how she feels. These strategies should be modeled and practiced, and feedback should be given to the child.
- Remember that even tantrums may be functional for a child, especially if tantrums are followed by adult compliance; be careful to avoid unwitting reinforcement.

27 Frequently irritable, "touchy," or fussy

- Record the frequency of a child's crying or whining. Use *differential reinforcement of other behavior* (DRO) by giving points or tokens and praise to the child for not crying or whining. Use *differential reinforcement of incompatible behavior* (DRI) by giving a sticker to the child each time she complies without any complaints.
- An infant who is colicky will fuss, cry, and be irritable for 3 hours or more, at least 3 days a week. You must cope with the distress until the infant outgrows it. Movement, noises, and tactile stimulation in the form of car rides, putting the baby seat on the washing machine while running, or walking may quiet the child.
- A back massager or tape recorder can calm a child. Pair the reinforcing activity with another activity that is not as enjoyable for the child. Use the reinforcer only if the child is calmly participating in the less desirable activity. If the child cries, remove the massager or tape recorder. When the child stops crying, return the reinforcer.

28 Can't wait at all for food or toy

- Require waiting for a very short time without fuss, then gradually increase the "wait" time, remembering to be encouraging and rewarding when the child waits without a fuss.
- Teach the child how to express his wants and needs in responsible ways. Teach the child how to use "I" messages to express his feelings. Use

role-play, modeling, practice, and precorrections. Warn the child that he may not get his way. Explain how the child can act appropriately, and give ongoing feedback during practice and real situations. A reward-and-consequence system can be set up for appropriate and inappropriate expressive behaviors. When redirection is given, it should be subtle, and frequent attention should be given to the child for appropriate behavior.

- *Learned helplessness* refers to children learning that they can do nothing on their own. Social-skills training in independence and proper ways to ask for help should be taught. When responding to inappropriate behaviors, be consistent. Reinforce all attempts the child makes to self-help.
- Use a token system to make changes more pleasant. Break the steps of transition into several parts, and give the child one point for each step followed correctly.

29 Demands attention continually

- *Learned helplessness* refers to children learning that they can do nothing on their own. Social-skills training in independence and proper ways to ask for help should be taught. When responding to inappropriate behaviors, be consistent. Reinforce all attempts the child makes to self-help.
- Teach the child how to express his or her wants and needs in responsible ways. Teach the child how to use "I" messages to express his feelings. Use role-play, modeling, practice, and precorrections. Warn the child that he may not get his way. Explain how the child can act appropriately, and give ongoing feedback during practice and real situations. A reward-and-consequence system can be set up for appropriate and inappropriate expressive behaviors. When redirection is given, it should be subtle, and frequent attention should be given to the child for appropriate behavior.

30 Controls adult's behavior, "is the boss"

- Teach the child how to express her wants and needs in responsible ways. Teach the child how to use "I" messages to express her feelings. Use role-play, modeling, practice, and precorrections. Warn the child that she may not get her way. Explain how the child can act appropriately, and give ongoing feedback during practice and real situations. A reward-and-consequence system can be set up for appropriate and inappropriate expressive behaviors. When redirection is given, it should be subtle, and frequent attention should be given to the child for appropriate behavior.
- When a child is displaying inappropriate social behaviors, redirect his focus and limit the amount of attention he receives. Praise the child for shaking hands or patting a friend on the back. Give intermittent rewards to the child during intervals when undesirable behaviors have not been displayed. Help the child to develop appropriate alternative behaviors on his own, and give the child ongoing feedback regarding his behaviors and progress.

31 Jealous too often

- Teach the child how to express her wants and needs in responsible ways. Teach the child how to use "I" messages to express her feelings. Use role-play, modeling, practice, and precorrections. Warn the child that she may not get her way. Explain how the child can act appropriately, and give ongoing feedback during practice and real situations. A reward-and-consequence system can be set up for appropriate and inappropriate expressive behaviors. When redirection is given, it should be subtle, and frequent attention should be given to the child for appropriate behavior.
- When a child is displaying inappropriate social behaviors, redirect his focus and limit the amount of attention he receives. Praise the child for shaking hands or patting a friend on the back. Give intermittent rewards to the child during intervals when undesirable behaviors have not been displayed. Help the child to develop appropriate alternative behaviors on his own, and give the child ongoing feedback regarding his behaviors and progress.
- Use *behavioral momentum*—initially give very easy-to-follow requests, followed by reinforcement. Gradually increase the required effort.

32 Mostly on the go, "in high gear"

- Parent counseling and training should be conducted. The family stress level should also be addressed.
- Accident prevention in the home should be addressed, including safety latches on drawers and cabinets and provision of durable, age-appropriate toys.
- With rare exception, medication for overactivity should not be given to a child younger than age 4.
- A home token system should be developed that includes 20 minutes of parent–child attention every day, reinforcement of appropriate play, response cost, and time-out.
- Have the child practice staying with an activity for increasing amounts of time; begin with small demands followed by reinforcement.

33 Doesn't sit still

- This behavior could be associated with attention-deficit/hyperactivity disorder (ADHD). If this is the case, a psychologist as well as a physician might be consulted.
- A home token system should be developed that includes 20 minutes of parent–child attention every day, reinforcement of appropriate play, response cost, and time-out.
- Play a game of "Who can sit still longer?" and let the child win. Gradually increase the time.
- Offer rewards for staying in place for longer periods of time.

34 Too "grabby," impulsive

- This behavior could be associated with attention-deficit/hyperactivity disorder (ADHD). If this is the case, a psychologist as well as a physician might be consulted.
- A home token system should be developed that includes 20 minutes of parent–child attention every day, reinforcement of appropriate play, response cost, and time-out.
- Reward the child for refraining from grabbing while asking for the wanted object.

35 Almost always refuses to do what is told

- Look at the child, smile, and use a pleasant tone of voice when giving instructions. Give as few instructions as possible. The fewer you give, the more instructions the child will follow. Give instructions that the child can follow, asking for positive action rather than pointing out negative behavior. Instead of asking the child to stop doing something, ask him or her to engage in a substitute positive behavior. Do not repeat instructions. Wait 1 minute (or another amount of specified time), and call time-out if the child has not done what was asked, or subtract a half hour from her bedtime. When the child does what is asked, tell her what she did that you liked. Give instructions only when you are willing and able to follow up on the child's compliance or noncompliance.
- Establish eye contact, say the child's name, and state the desired behavior in a business-like manner. If the child does not comply in about 5 seconds, repeat the direction and gesture or use a small physical prompt. Ignore any further noncompliance (except in dangerous situations). When the child does what is requested, praise him immediately in an enthusiastic manner.
- Combining a token system with a self-evaluation system (e.g., circling a specified number of smiley faces on a card) should help to generalize compliance. The child's rating is compared with the adult's rating (i.e., the token system). The child receives extra tokens if his rating is within 1 point of the adult's.
- Immediately before asking the child to do something she usually does not do when asked, request the child to perform three tasks that she usually enjoys doing. Each request should be given within 5 seconds after the child complies, along with praise.
- Encourage the child to "beat the buzzer" in completing a task.
- Videotape the child exhibiting both compliant and noncompliant behavior. Review the videotape with the child, discussing whether what he did was appropriate, followed by role-playing.
- Intervention for preschool children who are noncompliant may involve a parent-training program teaching parents differential attentional skills, time-out, and other techniques. One such program is Eyberg's Parent–Child Interaction Therapy (PCIT) (Eyberg & Robinson, 1982). PCIT consists of two parts—child-directed interaction and parent-directed inter-

action—both occurring during paired play situations. The focus of PCIT is not only to decrease the noncompliant or undesirable behavior but also to increase other, more socially acceptable behaviors.

- Inappropriate behaviors that persist over time may serve a communicative function for the child, such as expressing boredom, frustration with tasks that are too difficult, lack of understanding of directions, desire for something, or the wish to avoid something. Determine the function of the behavior, and plan strategies to prevent the target behavior from occurring. Interventions to be considered in a child care or preschool environment may include rearranging the environment (e.g., large, open spaces may encourage running); designing varied developmentally appropriate activities and materials; maintaining a consistent schedule; structuring transitions; and modeling appropriate behaviors. Consider information about behaviors that occur in other environments, and include the child's family when designing and implementing interventions.
- A family ecology approach to behavioral interventions is more effective than a traditional mental health agency approach. Such a broad-based intervention plan includes the child, the family, and peer interactions and offers individualized support such as parent management training, problem-solving skills training, social-skills training, or behavior therapy.

36 Throws or breaks things on purpose

- The child may break things to find out what happens. Develop science activities that allow the child to experiment with dropping various items, and then discuss the effects. Teach the child that breaking things is okay only during designated activities.
- Inappropriate behaviors that persist over time may serve a communicative function for the child, such as expressing boredom, frustration with tasks that are too difficult, lack of understanding of directions, desire for something, or the wish to avoid something. Determine the function of the behavior, and plan strategies to prevent the target behavior from occurring. Interventions to be considered in a child care or preschool environment may include rearranging the environment (e.g., large, open spaces may encourage running); designing varied developmentally appropriate activities and materials; maintaining a consistent schedule; structuring transitions; and modeling appropriate behaviors. Consider information about behaviors that occur in other environments, and include the child's family when designing and implementing interventions.
- Combining a token system with a self-evaluation system (e.g., circling a specified number of smiley faces on a card) should help to generalize compliance. The child's rating is compared with the adult's rating (i.e., the token system). The child receives extra tokens if her rating is within 1 point of the adult's.

37 Bites, hits, kicks others

- Teach and model appropriate ways that hands, arms, feet, and legs are used. The child should actively participate in the learning activities.

- Teach the child alternative solutions to disagreements, using dolls to model appropriate behaviors resulting in cooperation and subsequent rewards; use contracts, planned ignoring, and reinforcement of appropriate behaviors.
- When a child is displaying inappropriate social behaviors, redirect his focus and limit the amount of attention he receives. Praise the child for shaking hands or patting a friend on the back. Give intermittent rewards to the child during intervals when undesirable behaviors have not been displayed. Help the child to develop appropriate alternative behaviors on his own, and give the child ongoing feedback regarding his behaviors and progress.
- If a child is endangering others, clear all other children from the room. Prior to any incidents, determine consequences for the behaviors, and teach the child self-control strategies. Use physical restraint only when necessary, and say the child's name in stating verbal instructions and when giving him redirection.
- Any threat made by a child should be taken seriously. Let the child know that you are available to talk about anything and that her threat is a serious concern. Praise the child when she is not making threats, and give her frequent attention. Explain to the child the meaning of a threat, and teach appropriate alternative behaviors.
- Teach the child about self-image and self-control strategies. Give the child ongoing feedback regarding his behavior.

Resources

Following is a list of resources that give more detailed information on intervention strategies related to *Hyper-sensitive/active* problems. Full citations can be found in the reference list at the end of the manual.

Bech (1993).
Bell (1986).
Blackman & Silberman (1971).
Blechman (1985).
Kadzin (1987).
Lyman & Hembree-Kigin (1994).
Sprick & Howard (1995).
Strain & Hemmeter (1997).
Trad (1989).

UNDERREACTIVE ITEMS

38 Rarely smiles, giggles, or laughs at funny things

- Children learn to laugh when shown a laughing model. Listen to a funny audiotape or watch a funny videotape with your child, and model appropriate laughing and smiling.

- A child's frequent complaints should be ignored. Changing the subject is a good way to stop a child from talking about depressing topics. Listening to a child and commenting only after she changes the subject is a way to limit complaining. Praising a child for problem solving may help her focus on the positive.
- If a child seems lonely, parents can set good examples of how to make friends. Teach the child about eye contact, smiling, and being a good listener. Model friendliness to others.
- Provide children with an opportunity to entertain friends at home. Do not choose your child's friends.
- When a child is sad, talk to him about those feelings, but try to discuss the sadness at a time when he is not acting sad (do not encourage sadness through your immediate attention to it). Let the child know he is valued.
- If a child is displaying apathetic or sad behavior, depression should be considered, and perhaps a psychologist should be consulted.

39 Doesn't pay attention to sights and sounds

- Pervasive developmental disorder (PDD) is associated with lack of attention to the environment. Explore the environment with the child. Model appropriate eye contact, facial expression, and physical gesturing.
- Use brief teaching sessions to teach the child how to maintain his or her attention. Praise the child for paying attention, and ask the child questions periodically.
- Assuming no hearing loss is present, combined neurodevelopmental and sensory integration strategies used by trained parents have resulted in improvements in their children with multiple disabilities to respond to toys. Sensory integration therapy is reported to improve attentional focus.

40 Doesn't seem to watch moving objects

- Pervasive developmental disorder (PDD) is associated with lack of attention to the environment. Explore the environment with the child. Model appropriate eye contact, facial expression, and physical gesturing.
- Use brief teaching sessions to teach the child how to maintain his attention. Praise the child for paying attention, and ask the child questions periodically. Little attention should be given to the child when the child is acting apathetically. Behavior that is appropriate for the situation should be reinforced.

41 Shows no surprise to new events

- Pervasive developmental disorder (PDD) is associated with lack of attention to the environment. Explore the environment with the child. Model appropriate eye contact, facial expression, and physical gesturing.
- Use brief teaching sessions to teach the child how to maintain his or her attention. Praise the child for paying attention, and ask the child questions periodically.

- If a child is displaying apathetic behavior, depression should be considered, and perhaps a psychologist should be consulted.
- Little attention should be given to the child when the child is acting apathetically. Behavior that is appropriate for the situation should be reinforced.

42 Doesn't react to own name

- A child displaying this behavior should be checked for hearing difficulty and depression. A consultation with a psychologist might be considered.
- Ask the child to repeat short statements and explain what the statements mean.
- Pervasive developmental disorder (PDD) is associated with lack of attention to the environment. Explore the environment with the child. Model appropriate eye contact, facial expression, and physical gesturing.
- Use brief teaching sessions to teach the child how to maintain his or her attention. Praise the child for paying attention, and ask the child questions periodically.

43 Doesn't care when others are hurt

- Role-play, dolls, and puppets can be used to dramatize the importance of empathy. Have the child practice showing concern when someone is hurt.
- When a child is displaying inappropriate social behaviors, redirect her focus and limit the amount of attention she receives. Praise the child for shaking hands or patting a friend on the back. Give intermittent rewards to the child during intervals when undesirable behaviors have not been displayed. Help the child to develop appropriate alternative behaviors on her own, and give the child ongoing feedback regarding her behaviors and progress.
- Pervasive developmental disorder (PDD) is associated with lack of attention to the environment. Explore the environment with the child. Model appropriate eye contact, facial expression, and physical gesturing.
- Use brief teaching sessions to teach the child how to maintain her attention. Praise the child for paying attention, and ask the child questions periodically.

44 Doesn't play much at all

- Pair two children who are already familiar with each other. Model sharing and joint play. Allow children to play, and praise them for joint play. If children are not playing together, use brief reminders.
- Take pictures of activity and peer choices. Allow the child to select an activity and playmates using the pictures. Model interactions, and praise the child's use of the pictures.

- Teach the child to play with simple games or objects for brief periods. Gradually increase the time and complexity of play. Some children do not naturally play, but must be encouraged to explore and play.
- Initiate a simple game with the child, such as Pat-a-Cake, Peek-a-Boo, Hot-Cold, or Hide and Seek. Make the initial activities easy and rewarding. Gradually reduce extrinsic rewards and encourage playing with you as the reward. Be sure to move ahead slowly, practicing the same play activities with gradual elaborations.

45 Doesn't enjoy playing with mother or caregiver

- Pair two children who are already familiar with each other. Model sharing and joint play. Allow children to play, and praise them for joint play. If children are not playing together, use brief reminders.
- Take pictures of activity and peer choices. Allow the child to select an activity and playmates using the pictures. Model interactions, and praise the child's use of the pictures.
- Structure some brief, simple playing, and follow that with the child's favorite activity or food. After awhile, playing with you will be rewarding in itself.
- Initiate a simple game with the child, such as Pat-a-Cake, Peek-a-Boo, Hot-Cold, or Hide and Seek. Make the initial activities easy and rewarding. Gradually reduce extrinsic rewards, and encourage playing with you as the reward. Be sure to move ahead slowly, practicing the same play activities with gradual elaborations.

46 Isn't upset when toy is taken away

- Initiate a simple game with the child, such as Pat-a-Cake, Peek-a-Boo, Hot-Cold, or Hide and Seek. Make the initial activities easy and rewarding. Gradually reduce extrinsic rewards, and encourage playing with you as the reward. Be sure to move ahead slowly, practicing the same play activities with gradual elaborations.
- Pair two children who are already familiar with each other. Model sharing and joint play. Allow children to play, and praise them for joint play. If children are not playing together, use brief reminders.
- Take pictures of activity and peer choices. Allow the child to select an activity and playmates using the pictures. Model interactions, and praise the child's use of the pictures.
- Pervasive developmental disorder (PDD) is associated with lack of attention to the environment. Explore the environment with the child. Model appropriate eye contact, facial expression, and physical gesturing.
- Use brief teaching sessions to teach the child how to maintain his or her attention. Praise the child for paying attention, and ask the child questions periodically.
- If a child is displaying apathetic behavior, depression should be considered, and perhaps a psychologist should be consulted.

- Little attention should be given to the child when acting apathetically. Behavior that is appropriate for the situation should be reinforced.

47 Almost never babbles or tries to talk

- If the child talks in one environment but not another (e.g., talks at home but not at school), an intervention plan that begins with modeling, successive approximations, and continuous reinforcement (e.g., praise and candy) in an initial session can be used. In following sessions, secondary reinforcers and variable-interval schedules can be employed. Gradually, the plan should be generalized to other locations and with other people and children.
- For children with *reluctant speech* (i.e., will speak in all environments if motivated enough) or who are electively mute, interventions include social and tangible reinforcement, shaping and fading, and response cost.
- Use prompts (nonverbal, verbal), modeling (e.g., say, "Want drink?"), and praise to encourage the use of verbal language in natural environments. Providing interesting materials (some out of reach), presenting choices, acting in an absurd manner, and creating situations where the child will need assistance all help to increase verbal language.
- If the child seems to be incapable of using anything other than a whiny voice, consult a speech-language pathologist. Use a tape recorder to teach the child the difference between his "grown-up" voice and his "not-grown-up" voice. Planned ignoring may also help to decrease the child's use of a whiny voice.

48 Doesn't react to sounds

- A child displaying this behavior should be checked for hearing difficulty and depression. A consultation with a psychologist might be considered.
- Assuming no hearing loss is present, combined neurodevelopmental and sensory integration strategies used by trained parents have resulted in improvements in their children with multiple disabilities to respond to toys. Sensory integration therapy can improve attentional focus.
- Pervasive developmental disorder (PDD) is associated with lack of attention to the environment. Explore the environment with the child. Model appropriate eye contact, facial expression, and physical gesturing.
- Use brief teaching sessions to teach the child how to maintain his or her attention. Praise the child for paying attention, and ask the child questions periodically.

Resources

Following is a list of resources that give more detailed information on intervention strategies related to *Underreactive* problems. Full citations can be found in the reference list at the end of the manual.

Bech (1993).
Blackman & Silberman (1971).

Blechman (1985).
Brown (1980).
Kurtz, Dowrick, Levy, & Batshaw (1996).
Lyman & Hembree-Kigin (1994).
Norton (1975).
Sprick & Howard (1995).
Trad (1989).

DYSREGULATED ITEMS

49 Often cries too long

- When a child cries too long, it may be to get attention. Operant conditioning can be used to reduce the child's amount of crying. Ignore all inappropriate crying, and reinforce all appropriate responses to situations.
- The use of successive approximations can also be effective. Reinforce only verbal responses to situations, not crying, and slowly work until you are reinforcing the child for not getting upset at all.
- An infant who is colicky will fuss, cry, and be irritable for 3 hours or more, at least 3 days a week. You must cope with the distress until the infant outgrows it. Movement, noises, and tactile stimulation, such as car rides, putting the baby seat on an operating washing machine, or holding the infant while walking may help quiet the child.

50 Often frightened by dreams or the nighttime

- Nightlights can be effective at relieving some children's fears. Dreams should be explained to children, but parents should not stay and sleep with the child or let him come into their bed.
- Children should be given options that they can exercise to alleviate fears, such as turning on the light, getting a drink, or thinking about happy things. A pad and paper should be left next to the bed for the child to draw a picture of what she was afraid. Parents should help their child look under the bed for monsters, but this should be done only one time. Children should then be given a flashlight to look on their own.
- Parent mannerisms should be considered, as well as the possibility of a child being depressed when he or she is overly fearful. A consultation with a psychologist might be necessary.
- Let the child know that you are available to talk. If a child is acting nervous, react consistently. Redirect the child to what she should be doing. Teach relaxation, identification of oncoming stress, and coping strategies. Some examples of strategies are counting backward and practicing muscle relaxation.

51 Screams in sleep and can't be comforted

- When a child wakes up screaming, allow the episode to run its course. Intervene as little as possible and only to keep the child safe. Do not restrain the child, or the episode will get worse. Keeping a consistent sleep schedule will reduce the likelihood of future episodes.

- Let the child know that you are available to talk. If a child is acting nervous, react consistently. Redirect the child to what she should be doing. Teach relaxation, identification of oncoming stress, and coping strategies. Some examples of strategies are counting backward and practicing muscle relaxation.

52 Can't comfort self when upset

- When a child cries too long, it may be to get attention. Operant conditioning can be used to reduce the child's amount of crying. Ignore all inappropriate crying, and reinforce all appropriate responses to situations.
- The use of successive approximations can also be effective. Reinforce only verbal responses to situations, not crying, and slowly work toward reinforcing the child for not getting upset at all.
- When a child wakes up screaming, allow the episode to run its course. Intervene as little as possible and only to keep child safe. Do not restrain the child, or the episode will get worse. Keeping a consistent sleep schedule will reduce the likelihood of future episodes.
- When consoling a child, remember that you may be unwittingly encouraging her behavior. Brief time-outs may be helpful in allowing time for the child to regain composure.

53 Wakes up often and doesn't fall back asleep

- All children should have the same bedtime 7 days a week. A good guideline is 7:00 P.M. for ages 3–4 and 7:30 P.M. for ages 5–7. The bedtime area should be quiet, and parents should set a good example by going to sleep in their bed and not falling asleep on the couch. Parents must be consistent and ignore their child's whining. Young children who cannot tell time should be shown a clock each night and told the time. If a child is not in bed at bedtime, little or no attention should be given. Reinforce children when they have gone to bed at the correct time.
- For infants born prematurely, low-frequency auditory and kinesthetic stimulation have been used to soothe and increase sleep. A rocker bed should be paired with a recorded heartbeat. This stimulation has been found to increase sleep and weight gain in infants.
- If a child is having difficulty sleeping because of nighttime fears, nightlights are often effective in relieving these fears. Dreams should be explained to children, but parents should not stay and sleep with the child or let them come into their bed.

54 Doesn't have a regular sleep schedule

- Children should have a routine bedtime 7 days a week. A good guideline is 7:00 P.M. for ages 3–4 and 7:30 P.M. for ages 5–7. The bedtime area should be quiet, and parents should set a good example by going to sleep in their bed and not falling asleep on the couch. Parents must be consistent and ignore their child's whining. Young children who cannot tell time should be shown a clock each night and told the time. If a child is not in bed at bedtime, little or no attention should be given. Reinforce children when they have gone to bed at the correct time.

- For infants born prematurely, low-frequency auditory and kinesthetic stimulation have been used to soothe and increase sleep. A rocker bed should be paired with a recorded heartbeat. This stimulation has been found to increase sleep and weight gain in infants.
- If a child is having difficulty sleeping because of nighttime fears, nightlights are often effective in relieving these fears. Dreams should be explained to children, but parents should not stay and sleep with the child or let them come into their bed.

55 Too often needs help to fall asleep

- Children should have a routine bedtime 7 days a week. A good guideline is 7:00 P.M. for ages 3–4 and 7:30 P.M. for ages 5–7. The bedtime area should be quiet, and parents should set a good example by going to sleep in their bed and not falling asleep on the couch. Parents must be consistent and ignore their child's whining. Young children who cannot tell time should be shown a clock each night and told the time. If a child is not in bed at bedtime, little or no attention should be given to him or her. Reinforce children when they have gone to bed at the correct time.
- For infants born prematurely, low-frequency auditory and kinesthetic stimulation have been used to soothe and increase sleep. A rocker bed should be paired with a recorded heartbeat. This stimulation has been found to increase sleep and weight gain in infants.
- If a child is having difficulty sleeping because of nighttime fears, nightlights are often effective in relieving these fears. Dreams should be explained to children, but parents should not stay and sleep with the child or let them come into their bed.
- After storytime and putting the child to bed, try not to reenter the child's room; this typically encourages prolonged problems. Reward any improvements.

Resources

Following is a list of resources that give more detailed information on intervention strategies related to *Dysregulated* problems. Full citations can be found in the reference list at the end of the manual.

Blackman & Silberman (1971).
Blechman (1985).
Lyman & Hembree-Kigin (1994).

TABS References

Aman, M.G., Werry, J.S., & Turbott, S.H. (1992). Behavior of children with seizures: Comparison with norms and effect of seizure type. *The Journal of Nervous and Mental Disease, 180,* 124–129.

American Educational Research Association (AERA). (1985). *Standards for educational and psychological tests.* Washington, DC: American Psychological Association and the National Council for Measurement in Education.

American Psychiatric Association (APA). (1994). *Diagnostic and statistical manual of mental disorders* (4th ed.). Washington, DC: Author.

Amos, L.M. (1986). *The Baby Atypical Behavior Index (BABI): Research justification for item inclusion.* Unpublished doctoral dissertation, The Pennsylvania State University, University Park.

Bagnato, S.J. (1998). Diagnostic classifications: 0–3 [Invited review of the book *Diagnostic classification of mental health and developmental disorders of infancy and early childhood*]. *Journal of Psychoeducational Assessment, 16*(2), 1–3.

Bagnato, S.J., & Feldman, H. (1989). Closed head injury in infants and preschool children: Research and practice issues. *Infants and Young Children, 2*(1), 1–13.

Bagnato, S.J., & Neisworth, J.T. (1990). *System to Plan Early Childhood Services (SPECS).* Circle Pines, MN: American Guidance Service.

Baker, B.S. (1982). The use of music with autistic children. In E.W. Bell (Ed.), *Autism: A reference book* (pp. 93–96). White Plains, NY: Addison Wesley Longman.

Banks, S. (1997). *Caregivers and professional perceptions of assessment practices and validity for American Indian/Alaska native families.* Unpublished doctoral dissertation, The Pennsylvania State University, University Park.

Bates, J.E., & Wachs, T.D. (1994). *Temperament: Individual differences at the interface of biology and behavior.* Washington, DC: American Psychological Association.

Baumgardner, T.L., Reiss, A.L., Freund, L.A., & Abrams, M.T. (1995). Specification of the neurobehavioral phenotype in males with fragile X syndrome. *Pediatrics, 95*(5), 744–752.

Bayley, N. (1969). *Bayley Scales of Infant Development.* San Antonio, TX: Psychological Corporation.

Bech, R. (1993). *Project Ride for preschoolers.* Longmont, CO: Sopris West.

Bell, E.W. (1986). Reducing inappropriate behavior in autistic children. In E.W. Bell (Ed.), *Autism: A reference book* (pp. 93–96). White Plains, NY: Addison Wesley Longman.

Blackman, G.J., & Silberman, A. (1971). *Modification of child behavior.* Belmont, CA: Wadsworth.

Blackman, J.A., Westervelt, V.D., Stevenson, R., & Welch, A. (1991). Management of preschool children with attention deficit-hyperactivity disorder. *Topics in Early Childhood Special Education, 11*(2), 91–104.

Blechman, E.A. (1985). *Solving child behavior problems: At home and at school.* Champaign, IL: Research Press.

Brown, G.E. (1980). The effects of laughing vs. non-laughing model on humor responses in preschool children. *Journal of Experimental Psychology, 29*(2), 334–339.

Brunquell, P.J. (1994). Listening to epilepsy. *Infants and Young Children, 7*(1), 24–33.

Burgess, D.M., & Streissguth, A.P. (1990). Educating students with fetal alcohol syndrome or fetal alcohol effects. *Pennsylvania Reporter, 22*(1), 1–5.

Campbell, S.B. (1990). *Behavior problems in preschool children.* New York: Guilford Press.

Caplan, R., Guthrie, D., Shields, W.D., Sigman, M., Mundy, P., Sherman, T., & Vinters, H.V. (1992). Early onset intractable seizures: Nonverbal communication after hemispherectomy. *Developmental and Behavioral Pediatrics, 13*(5), 348–355.

Capone, A.M. (1988). *A retrospective study of atypical infant and toddler behavior.* Unpublished doctoral dissertation, The Pennsylvania State University, University Park.

Chapman, J.K., Worthington, L.A., Cook, M.J., & Mayfield, P.W. (1992). Cocaine-exposed infants: A potential generation of at-risk and vulnerable children. *The Transdisciplinary Journal, 2*(3), 223–237.

Chess, S., & Thomas, A. (1986). *Temperament in clinical practice.* New York: Guilford Press.

Clark, R., Paulson, A., & Conlin, S. (1993). Assessment of developmental status and parent–infant relationships: The therapeutic process of evaluation. In C. Zeanah (Ed.), *Handbook of infant mental health* (pp. 191–209). New York: Guilford Press.

Cooper, J.O., Heron, T.E., & Heward, W.L. (1987). *Applied behavior analysis.* Upper Saddle River, NJ: Prentice-Hall.

Cronbach, L. (1951). Coefficient alpha and the internal structure of tests. *Psychometrika, 16,* 297–334.

DeGangi, G.A. (1991a). Assessment of sensory, emotional, and attentional problems in regulatory disordered infants: Part 1. *Infants and Young Children, 3*(3), 1–8.

DeGangi, G.A. (1991b). Treatment of sensory, emotional and attentional problems in regulatory disordered infants: Part 2. *Infants and Young Children, 3*(3), 9–19.

Diamond, K., & Squires, J. (1993). The role of parental report in the screening and assessment of young children. *Journal of Early Intervention, 17*(2), 107–115.

Dilts, C.V., Carey, J.C., Kircher, J.C., Hoffman, R.O., Creel, D., Ward, K., Clark, E., & Leonard, C.O. (1996). Children and adolescents with neurofibromatosis 1: A behavioral phenotype. *Developmental and Behavioral Pediatrics, 17*(4), 229–239.

Dunst, C.J., Jenkins, V., & Trivette, C.M. (1988). Family Support Scale. In C.J. Dunst, C.M. Trivette, & A.G. Deal (Eds.), *Enabling and empowering families: Principles and guidelines for practice* (pp. 155–157). Cambridge, MA: Brookline Books.

Dykens, E.M., Hodapp, R.M., & Leckman, J.F. (1994). *Behavior and development in fragile X syndrome.* Thousand Oaks, CA: Sage Publications.

Einfeld, S.L., & Tonge, B.J. (1992). *Manual for the developmental behaviour checklist: Primary Care Version (DBC-P).* Randwick, Australia: The Prince of Wales Hospital.

Emde, R.N., Katz, E.L., & Thorpe, J.K. (1978). Emotional expression in infancy: Early deviations in Down's syndrome. In M. Lewis & L. Rosenblum (Eds.), *The development of affect: Genesis of behavior* (Vol. 1, pp. 351–360). New York: Plenum Press.

Eyberg, S.M., & Robinson, E. (1982). Parent–child interaction training: Effects on family functioning. *Journal of Clinical Child Psychology, 11,* 130–137.

Fellner, D.J., LaRoche, M., & Sulzer-Azaroff, B. (1984). The effects of adding interruption to differential reinforcement on targeted and novel self-stimulatory behaviors. *Journal of Behavior Therapy and Experimental Psychiatry, 15*(4), 315–321.

Ferber, J. (1985). *Solve your child's sleep problems.* New York: Simon & Schuster.

Freund, L. (1994). Diagnosis and developmental issues for young children with fragile X syndrome. *Infants and Young Children, 6*(3), 34–35.

Gersh, E.S. (1991). Medical concerns and treatments. In E. Geralis (Ed.), *Children with cerebral palsy: A parents' guide* (pp. 57–61). Bethesda, MD: Woodbine House.

Glascoe, F.P. (1991). Developmental screening: Rationale, methods, and application. *Infants and Young Children, 4*(1), 1–10.

Glascoe, F.P., & MacLean, W.E. (1990). How parents appraise their child's development. *Family Relations, 39,* 280–283.

Greenspan, S.I. (1991). Regulatory disorders: Clinical perspectives. *NIDA Research Monograph, V*(114), 165–172.

Huntington, G.S., & Simeonsson, R.J. (1993). Temperament and adaptation in infants and young children with disabilities. *Infant Mental Health Journal, 14,* 49–60.

Huntley, R. (1991). *The sleep book for tired parents: Help for solving children's sleep problems.* Seattle: Parenting Press.

Kadzin, A.E. (1987). Treatment of antisocial behavior in children: Current status and future directions. *Exceptional Children, 55*(5), 420–428.

Kern, L., Koegel, R.L., & Dunlap, G. (1984). The influence of vigorous versus mild exercise on autistic stereotyped behaviors. In E.W. Bell (Ed.), *Autism: A reference book* (pp. 93–96). White Plains, NY: Addison Wesley Longman.

Kopp, C.B. (1982). Antecedents of self-regulation: A developmental perspective. *Developmental Psychology, 18*(2), 99–214.

Kurtz, L.A., Dowrick, P.W., Levy, S.E., & Batshaw, M.L. (1996). *Handbook of developmental disabilities: Resources for interdisciplinary care.* Gaithersburg, MD: Aspen.

Lester, B.M., Corwin, M.J., Sepkoski, C., Seifer, R., Peucker, M., McLaughlin, S., & Golub, H.L. (1991). Neurobehavioral syndromes in cocaine-exposed newborn infants. *Child Development, 62,* 694–705.

Lester, B.M., Tronick, E., & Mayes, L. (1993). *A neurobehavioral consortium on early cocaine exposure.* Paper presented at the annual meeting of the American Academy of Pediatrics, Boston, MA.

Lovaas, O.I. (1981). *Teaching developmentally disabled children.* Austin, TX: PRO-ED.

Lyman, R.D., & Hembree-Kigin, T. (1994). *Mental health interventions with preschool children.* New York: Plenum Press.

McIntosh, D.E., & Cole-Love, A.S. (1996). Profile comparisons between ADHD and non-ADHD children on the Temperament Assessment Battery for Children. *Journal of Psychoeducational Assessment, 14,* 362–372.

Neisworth, J.T., & Bagnato, S.J. (1996). Assessment for early intervention: Emerging themes and practices. In S. Odom & M. McLean (Eds.), *Early intervention/early childhood special education: Recommended practices* (pp. 23–58). Austin, TX: PRO-ED.

Neisworth, J.T., Bagnato, S.J., & Salvia, J. (1995). Neurobehavioral markers for early regulatory disorders. *Infants and Young Children, 8*(1), 8–17.

Norton, Y. (1975). Neurodevelopment and sensory integration for the profoundly retarded multiply handicapped child. *The American Journal of Occupational Therapy, 29*(2), 93–100.

Phelps, L., & Grabowski, J. (1992). Fetal alcohol syndrome: Diagnostic features and psychoeducational risk factors. *School Psychology Quarterly, 7*(2), 112–128.

Rogers, S.J., & D'Eugenio, D.B. (1981). Developmental Programming for Infants and Young Children (DPIYC): Vol. 2. Early Intervention Developmental Profile (EIDP). Ann Arbor: University of Michigan Press.

Rothbart, M.K., & Ahadi, S.A. (1994). Temperament and the development of personality. *Journal of Abnormal Psychology, 103,* 55–66.

Rothbart, M.K., & Derryberry, D. (1981). Development of individual differences in temperament. In M.E. Lamb & A.L. Brown (Eds.), *Advances in developmental psychology* (Vol. 1., pp. 37–86). Mahwah, NJ: Lawrence Erlbaum Associates.

Rothbart, M.K., & Derryberry, D. (1982). Theoretical issues in temperament. In M. Lewis & L. Taft (Eds.), *Developmental disabilities: Theory, assessment, and intervention* (pp. 383–400). Jamaica, NY: SP Medical and Scientific Books.

Rutter, S.C., & Cole, T.R.P. (1991). Psychological characteristics of Sotos syndrome. *Developmental Medicine and Child Neurology, 33,* 898–902.

Salvia, J., & Good, R. (1982). Significant discrepancies in the classification of pupils: Differentiating the concept. In J.T. Neisworth (Ed.), *Assessment in special education* (pp. 77–82). Gaithersburg, MD: Aspen.

Salvia, J., & Ysseldyke, J.E. (1998). *Assessment in special and remedial education* (7th ed.). Boston, MA: Houghton Mifflin.

Schopler, E. (1986). *Childhood Autism Rating Scale: CARS.* Los Angeles: Western Psychological Services.

Siegel, B. (1994). *Developmentally-operationalized definitions: DSM-IV criteria for autistic disorder.* San Francisco: University of California at San Francisco Developmental Disorders Clinic.

Siegel, B. (1996). *The world of the autistic child.* New York: Oxford University Press.

Sprick, R.S., & Howard, L.M. (1995). *The teacher's encyclopedia of behavior management: 100 problems/500 plans.* Longmont, CO: Sopris West.

Stake, R., & Wardrop, J. (1971). Gain score errors in performance contracting. *Research in the Teaching of English, 5,* 226–229.

Strain, P.S., & Hemmeter, M.L. (1997). Keys to being successful when confronted with challenging behaviors. *Young Exceptional Children, 1*(1), 2–8.

Streissguth, A.P. (1997). *Fetal alcohol syndrome: A guide for families and communities.* Baltimore: Paul H. Brookes Publishing Co.

Streissguth, A.P., Herman, C.S., & Smith, D.W. (1978). Intelligence, behavior, and dysmorphogenesis in the fetal alcohol syndrome: A report on 20 patients. *The Journal of Pediatrics, 92*(3), 363–367.

Suen, H.K., Logan, C., Neisworth, J.T., & Bagnato, S.J. (1995). Parent–professional congruence: Is it necessary? *Journal of Early Intervention, 19*(3), 257–266.

Thomas, A., & Chess, S. (1977). *Temperament and development.* New York: Brunner/Mazel.

Thomas, J.M., & Tidmarsh, L. (1997). Hyperactive and disruptive behaviors in very young children: Diagnosis and intervention. *Infants and Young Children, 9*(3), 46–55.

Thorndike, R. (1963). *The concepts of over- and under-achievement.* New York: Columbia University Press.

Tome, S.A., Williamson, N.K., & Pauli, R.M. (1990). Temperament in Williams syndrome. *American Journal of Medical Genetics, 36,* 345–352.

Trad, P.V. (1989). *The preschool child: Assessment, diagnosis, and treatment* (pp. 542–564). New York: John Wiley & Sons.

U.S. Department of Education (1992). *Fourteenth Annual Report to Congress on the Implementation of the Individuals with Disabilities Education Act.* Washington, DC: Government Printing Office.

Vacca, J. (1995). *The perceived utility of developmental assessment instruments in the evaluation of infants and young children with presumed and/or authenticated neurological impairments.* Unpublished doctoral dissertation, The Pennsylvania State University, University Park.

Van Acker, R.V. (1991). Rett syndrome: A review of current knowledge. *Journal of Autism and Developmental Disorders, 21*(4), 381–406.

Watters, R.G., & Wood, D.E. (1983). Play and self-stimulatory behaviors of autistic and other severely dysfunctional children with different classes of toys. In E.W. Bell (Ed.), *Autism: A reference book* (pp. 93–96). White Plains, NY: Addison Wesley Longman.

Welteroth, S. (1998). *Reliability study of temperament and regulatory indicators of atypical development in young children.* Unpublished manuscript, The Pennsylvania State University, University Park.

Wolery, M., Bailey, D.B., & Sugai, G.M. (1988). *Effective teaching: Principles and procedures of applied behavior analysis with exceptional students.* Needham Heights, MA: Allyn & Bacon.

Wolery, M., & Fleming, L.A. (1993). Implementing individualized curricula in integrated settings. In C.A. Peck, S.L. Odom, & D.D. Bricker (Eds.), *Integrating young children with disabilities into community programs: Ecological perspectives on research and implementation* (pp. 109–132). Baltimore: Paul H. Brookes Publishing Co.

World Health Organization. (1989). *International classification of diseases: Vol. 1. Clinical modification* (9th ed.). Ann Arbor, MI: Commission on Professional and Hospital Activities.

ZERO TO THREE: National Center for Infants, Toddlers, and Families. (1994). *Diagnostic classification: 0–3.* Washington, DC: Author.

Zimmermann, I.L., Steiner, V.C., & Pond, K.E. (1979). *Preschool Language Scale.* San Antonio, TX: Psychological Corporation.

TABS Appendix

AGENCIES AND ORGANIZATIONS CONTRIBUTING TO THE TABS SAMPLE

Alabama

FOCUS, Inc., Chuyiak

Arkansas

AR CARES/University of Arkansas Medical School, Little Rock
Preschool Special Services, Northeast Arkansas School District, Paragould

California

Citrus College Child Development Center, Glendora
HOPE Infant Family Support Program, San Diego

Colorado

Child Find, Denver
Child Find/Early Childhood, Aurora
Early Childhood Center, Westminster
Monfort Kindergarten, Greeley

District of Columbia

Children's National Medical Center, Department of Medical Genetics, Washington

Florida

Child Development Path, Fort Lauderdale
The Children's Medical Center at St. Mary's, Child Development Center, West Palm Beach
Developmental Evaluation and Intervention Program, Melbourne

Georgia

Marcus Center, Atlanta
The Pediatric Center, Stone Mountain

Illinois

Franklin-Williamson Youth Services Bureau, West Frankfurt
Lakeview Early Intervention Program, Chicago
LeMoyne School, Chicago

Iowa

Heartland Area Education Agency II, Ames

Kansas

The Capper Foundation, Topeka
Parents-As-Teachers, Waterville
Valley Park Elementary School, Overland Park

Kentucky

University of Kentucky, Kentucky Early Intervention System, Lexington

Maryland

Infant Toddler Program, Bel Air
The Johns Hopkins Hospital, Developmental Pediatrics, Baltimore
Kennedy Krieger Institute, Baltimore

Massachusetts

Brighton-Dimock Early Intervention Program, Roxbury
Weston Public Schools, Weston

Michigan

Ingham Intermediate School District, Division of Special Education, Mason
University of Michigan Medical Center, Taubman Center, Ann Arbor

Minnesota

Beaumont Hospital, Center for Human Development, Berkley Medical Center, Berkley
Early Intervention Program/Community Education, Independent School District #197, West St. Paul
Early Childhood Services, Center/Zachary Square, Maple Grove

Missouri

Gillis Center, Kansas City
Howard Park Early Intervention Center, Ellisville
Kirkwood School District R-7, Kirkwood
North Kansas City School District, Pleasant Valley
State of Missouri, Department of Elementary and Secondary Education, St. Louis
United Services, St. Peters

Nebraska

Papillion-LaVista Public Schools, LaVista

New Mexico

Southwest Communication Resources, Bernalillo

New Jersey

Children's Center for Therapy and Learning, Inc., Cedar Knolls

New York

Beginnings Early Intervention Program, Schenectady
Early Start, Brooklyn

Ohio

Lorain County General Health District, Elyria

Oklahoma

Oklahoma State Department of Health, Sooner Start Early Intervention, Oklahoma City

Oregon

Relief Nursery, Inc., Eugene
Statewide Regional Autism Services, Linn-Benton Education Service District, Albany

Pennsylvania

Blair County Children's Center, Altoona
Center for Educational Diagnosis and Remediation (CEDAR) Day Care Center, University Park
Cen-Clear Child Services, Philipsburg
Central Intermediate Unit #10, West Decatur
Central Susquehanna Intermediate Unit Early Intervention Program, Montandon
Central Susquehanna Intermediate Unit #16, Lewisburg
Central Allegheny Intermediate Unit 15, Summerdale
Child and Family Studies, Allegheny-Singer Research Institute (ASRI), Pittsburgh
Child Development Unit, Children's Hospital of Pittsburgh, Pittsburgh
Easter Seal Society of Centre-Clinton Counties, State College
Easter Seals, Baby Step Program, Pittsburgh
Edinboro University, Edinboro
Imagination Station Daycare Center, State College
Infant Evaluation Program, Inc., State College
Learning Station, State College
Northeastern Intermediate Unit #19, Moscow
Northeastern Intermediate Unit #19, Clark Summit
Northumberland Area Head Start Program, Sunbury
Snyder, Union, Mifflin Child Development, Inc., Lewisburg
Snyder, Union, Mifflin Counties Head Start Program, Lewisburg
St. Peter's Child Development Center, Pittsburgh
Western Psychiatric Institute and Clinic, John Merck Multiple Disabilities Program, University of Pittsburgh, Pittsburgh

Rhode Island

Rhode Island Hospital, Child Development Center, Providence

South Carolina

University of South Carolina, School of Medicine, Department of Neuropsychiatry and Behavioral Science, Columbia

Tennessee

Quality Pediatric Care, Hendersonville
University of Memphis, Memphis

Texas

Abilene Regional Mental Health/Mental Retardation Center, Advancing Babies Chances, Abilene
Amarillo State Center, Early Childhood Intervention Program, Amarillo
Andrews Center, Andrews Early Childhood Intervention Program, Tyler
Austin-Travis County Mental Health/Mental Retardation Center, Austin Infant Parent Program, Austin
BABYTRACKS Project, Easter Seal Society-Trinity, Carrollton
Beaumont State Center, First Steps, Beaumont
Brenham State School, Know Infant Delays, Bellville
Capital Area Easter Seals Rehabilitation Center, Pediatric Development Program, Austin
CEDEN of Austin, Parent Child Program, Austin
Child Development Program, Fort Worth
Collin County Mental Health/Mental Retardation Center, Early Childhood Intervention Program, McKinney
Corpus Christi State School, Bay to Bay Infant Development Program, Corpus Christi
Dallas Center for the Developmentally Disabled, Dallas
Dallas County Mental Health/Mental Retardation Center, Parent Infant Training Center, Dallas
Deep East Texas Regional Mental Health/Mental Retardation Services, Cornerstone, Crockett
Early Childhood Intervention, Sabine Valley Center, Longview
Early Childhood Intervention—Mental Health/Mental Retardation, Austin
El Paso Rehabilitation Center, Community Service Program, El Paso
Heart of Texas Region Mental Health/Mental Retardation Center, Klaras Children's Center, Waco
Johnson County Mental Health/Mental Retardation—Early Childhood Intervention, Child Development Program, Cleburne
Klein Instructional Services Division, Project Keep Pace, Klein
Life Management Center for Mental Health/Mental Retardation Services, Child Development Services, El Paso
Lubbock Instructional Services Division, DEBT'S Early Childhood Intervention Project, Lubbock
Mexia State School, Step by Step, Mexia

North Texas Easter Seal Rehabilitation Center, Inc., Infant/Child Development Program, Wichita Falls
Nueces County Mental Health/Mental Retardation Community Center, Infant Development Program, Corpus Christi
Parent Infant Training Center, Dallas
Project Baby Care, Sabine Valley Center, Carrollton
Project First STEP, El Paso City—County Health District, El Paso
Project PRINT, Meyer Center for Developmental Pediatrics, Houston
Region 8 Education Service Center, Mt. Pleasant
Region 18 Education Service Center, Midland
Hidalgo County Health Department, RISC (Regional Infant Screening Consortium), Edinburg
San Antonio State School, Early Intervention Program, Uvalde
Silsbee Instructional Services Division, Project Search, Silsbee
Wichita General Hospital, STAR Project, Wichita Falls
Tarrant County Infant Tracking Project (TRACS), Cook–Fort Worth Children's Medical Center, Forth Worth
Early Childhood Intervention of Tarrant County, Tarrant County Mental Health/Mental Retardation Services, Fort Worth
Texacoma, Mental Health/Mental Retardation Services, Project KIND, Denison
Texarkana Special Education Opportunities, Inc., Valued Infants and Parents, Texarkana
Texas Department of Mental Health/Mental Retardation Services, Outreach Program, Denton
Texas Interagency Council on Early Childhood Intervention, Austin
Texas Scottish Rite Hospital for Children, Dallas
TINY TRAX, Any Baby Can of Texas, San Antonio

Utah

Children with Special Health Care Needs, Child Development Clinic, Salt Lake City

Vermont

Winston-Prouty Center for Child Development, Brattleboro

Virginia

Children's Hospital of Richmond, Education Department, Richmond
Children's Hospital of The King's Daughters, Norfolk
Northwestern Community Services, Winchester
Parent–Infant Education Program, Powmatan
Rappahannock Area Community Services Board, Fredericksburg
Rockbridge Area Community Services Board, RAISE Infant Program, Lexington

Washington

Birth to Three Developmental Center, Federal Way

West Virginia

Birth to Three Program, Maternal and Child Health, Charleston

Shawnee Hills Early Intervention, Charleston
Summit Center for Human Development, Sutton

International

Metropolitan Toronto Association for Community Living, Toronto and North York, Ontario, CANADA
Step-By-Step Early Learning Center, Kahnawake , Quebec, CANADA
Infant Development Program, Chilliwack, British Columbia, CANADA
Infant Development Program, Mission, British Columbia, CANADA
Child Development Project, Tynes Bay House, Devonshire, BERMUDA

CONVERSION TABLE

	TRI			Detached			Hyper-sensitive/ active			Underreactive			Dysregulated		
RS	%ile	*SS*	*SS*nd	%ile	*T-score*	*SS*nd	%ile	*T-score*	*SS*nd	%ile	*T-score*	*SS*nd	%ile	*T-score*	*SS*nd
0	84	113	115	65	55	54	77	58	57	60	54	53	61	54	53
1	61	109	104	23	47	42	46	53	49	15	42	40	15	42	40
2	48	104	99	13	39	38	32	48	45	6	31	34	5	29	34
3	37	100	96	6	31	35	22	44	42	2	19	30	2	16	30
4	28	95	91	3	23	32	14	39	39	1	7	28	<1	4	26
5	23	91	89	2	15	29	9	34	36	—	—	—	—	—	—
6	18	87	86	<1	7	26	6	29	34						
7	14	82	84	<1	0	24	3	25	31						
8	11	78	82	—	—	—	2	20	28						
9	8	73	79				<1	15	26						
10	6	69	76				—	—	—						
11	4	64	74												
12	3	60	71												
13	1	56	67												
14	<1	51	60												
15	—	—	—												

Note: N = 621 children not identified as having disabilities.

Conversion of raw scores *(RS)* to percentiles (%ile), standard scores *(SS)*, and T-scores, and standard scores normalized by area transformation (*SS*nd) for the *TRI* and subtests.

%ile: M = 100, *SD* = 15.

SS: M = 100, *SD* = 15.

T-score: M = 50. *SD* = 10.

*SS*nd: M = 50, *SD* = 10.

TABS Index

Page numbers followed by *f* indicate figures; those followed by *t* indicate tables.

Acquired brain injury, 2, 17, 36
Adaptability, 11, 14, 16, 36
ADHD, *see* Attention-deficit/hyperactivity disorder
Administering TABS Screener and TABS Assessment Tool, 4–5, 21–22
  completing background information, 22
  providing assistance, 22
  time required for completing, 22
Aggressive behavior, 14, 15, 85–86
AITBQ, *see* Atypical Infant and Toddler Behavior Questionnaire
Alertness, 2, 9
Anger, 72, 80
Anxiety, 11, 16
ASD, *see* Autism spectrum disorder
Assessment, 1, 2, 65–66, 68–69
  see also Temperament and Atypical Behavior Scale (TABS)
Attention-deficit/hyperactivity disorder (ADHD), 3, 10, 11, 13, 14, 71, 83
Attentional persistence, 9, 11, 16
Atypical behaviors, 1
  assessment of, 1, 65–66, 68–69; *see also* Temperament and Atypical Behavior Scale (TABS)
  collecting baseline data on, 66, 69
  communicative function of, 85
  definition of, 1
  frequency and intensity of, 1, 5–6
  identification of, 65, 68
  indicators of, 8
  intervention for, 63–93; *see also* Intervention
  neurobehavioral markers for, 8, 12–17
  in relation to same-age peers, 1
  risk/protective factors for, 65–66, 68–69
  target behaviors for TABS Assessment Tool, 5
  see also Temperament and self-regulation
Atypical development, 1, 8–9
Atypical Infant and Toddler Behavior Questionnaire (AITBQ), 35
Augmentative and alternative communication systems, 12
Autism spectrum disorder (ASD), 3, 5, 10, 11, 13–14
  indicators of, 8
  use of TABS for child with, 29–33, *29f–33f*, *29t*, *32t*

Babbling, 90
BABI, *see* Baby Atypical Behavior Inventory
Baby Atypical Behavior Inventory (BABI), 35
Bayley Scales of Infant Development, 26
Bedtime, 92–93
Behavior problems, *see* Atypical behaviors
Behavioral momentum, 83
Brain injury, 3, 17, 36

Categorization of TABS scores, 59–60
Cerebral gigantism, 17
Child abuse, 17
Child risk/protective factors, 65–66
Childhood Autism Rating Scale, 31
Cocaine exposure, prenatal, 10, 14
Coefficient alpha, 57
Communication problems, 13, 29, 90
Community-based, family-centered early intervention model, 64–67
  assess behavior, function, and risk/protective factors, 65–66, 68–69
  collect baseline data on problem behavior, 66, 69
  evaluate progress, 67, 70
  identify problem and restate it as goal, 65, 68
  implement intervention and ensure correct implementation, 67, 69–70
  monitor progress and implementation, 67, 70
  plan intervention, 66–67, 69
  specify objective for intervention, 66, 69
Conduct disorder, 10
Construct validity of TABS, 58–59, *60f*, *61f*, *61t*
Content validity of TABS, 57–58
Counterconditioning, 77
Crying, 2, 3, 26, 79–80, 91

DC:0–3, *see Diagnostic Classification: 0–3*
Defiant behavior, 3, 10, 14, 18, 71, 84–85

Depression, 74, 78, 87, 89
Derived scores, 44, 45*t*, 105*t*
accuracy of, 59–60
Desensitization, 76–77
Destructive behavior, 3, 85
Detached style of temperament, 3, 13
derived scores for, 105*t*
indicators of, 8
interventions for, 72–79
acts like others are not there, 73
consistently upset by changes in schedule, 72
disturbed by too much light, noise, or touching, 75–76
emotions don't match what is going on, 72
flaps hands over and over, 78
hardly ever starts on own to play with others, 73
makes strange throat noises, 75
moods and wants are too hard to figure out, 73–74
often stares into space, 74
overexcited in crowded places, 76–77
overly interested in toy/object, 77
plays with toys as if confused by how they work, 75
plays with toys in strange ways, 75
resists looking you in the eye, 73
seems to be in "own world," 74
seems to look through or past people, 72
shakes head over and over, 78
stares at lights, 77
"tunes out," loses contact with what is going on, 74–75
wanders around without purpose, 78
Development of TABS, 1, 35–49
item development, 35–40
55-item TABS Assessment Tool, 38–40, 38*f*, 39*t*–40*t*
final steps in item selection, 37–38
preliminary steps in item selection, 36–37
selecting items for TABS Screener, 40
norms, 40–44
characteristics of normative sample, 41, 42*t*
characteristics of sample of children with disabilities, 42–44, 44*t*, 45*t*
sampling procedures, 40–41
selecting normative sample of children without disabilities, 41
TABS performance of normative sample, 42, 42*t*, 43*t*
scores, 44–49
cutoff scores for TABS Screener, 25, 46, 49
derived scores, 44, 45*t*, 105*t*
score interpretation, 45–46, 46*f*–48*f*
Developmental milestones, 4
Developmental research, 7–20
Diagnostic and Statistical Manual of Mental Disorders, Fourth Edition (DSM-IV), 5, 14, 25, 31
Diagnostic Classification: 0–3 (DC:0–3), 10–12
TABS normative research as empirical validation of regulatory disorders axis of, 17–19, 19*t*
Differential reinforcement of incompatible (DRI) behavior, 73, 77, 80, 81
Differential reinforcement of lower levels, 78
Differential reinforcement of other (DRO) behavior, 73, 77, 78, 79, 81
"Difficult" styles of behavior, 10, 11
Disengagement, 2, 18
Distractibility, 14
Dreams, 91
DRI, *see* Differential reinforcement of incompatible behavior
DRO, *see* Differential reinforcement of other behavior
Drug exposure, prenatal, 10, 14–15, 36
DSM-IV, *see Diagnostic and Statistical Manual of Mental Disorders, Fourth Edition*
Dysregulated style of temperament, 3
derived scores for, 105*t*
interventions for, 91–93
can't comfort self when upset, 92
doesn't have a regular sleep schedule, 92–93
often cries too long, 91
often frightened by dreams or nighttime, 91
screams in sleep and cannot be comforted, 91–92
too often needs help to fall asleep, 93
wakes up often and does not fall back asleep, 92

Early intervention, *see* Intervention
Early Intervention Developmental Profile, 29
Eligibility for services, 1, 4, 36
TABS cutoff scores for, 25, 46, 49
Emotional intensity, 14, 72, 80
Environment
risk/protective factors for problem behaviors related to, 66
temperament and, 11–12
Epilepsy, 15, 74–75
Evaluating progress, 67, 70
Exercise, 77, 78

Extinction, 77
Extremes of temperament, 11–12

FAE, *see* Fetal alcohol effects
Family Support Scale, 30
FAS, *see* Fetal alcohol syndrome
Fearfulness, 11, 18, 91
Feeding problems, 11, 13, 15, 16, 26
Fetal alcohol effects (FAE), 14–15
Fetal alcohol syndrome (FAS), 5, 14–15
"Four A's of infancy," 10, 14
Fragile X syndrome, 5, 8, 13
Frustration intolerance, 15, 17, 80–81
Fussiness, 3, 10, 11, 81

Hyper-sensitive/active style of temperament, 3, 10, 12, 15, 18
  attention-deficit/hyperactivity disorder, 3, 10, 11, 13, 14, 71, 83
  derived scores for, 105*t*
  interventions for, 79–86
    almost always refuses to do what is told, 84–85
    bites, hits, kicks others, 85–86
    can't wait at all for food or toy, 81–82
    controls adult's behavior, "is the boss," 82
    demands attention continually, 82
    doesn't sit still, 83
    frequently irritable, "touchy," or fussy, 81
    gets angry too easily, 80
    has wide swings in mood, 80
    has wild temper tantrums, 81
    jealous too often, 83
    mostly on the go, "in high gear," 83
    often difficult to soothe when upset and crying, 79–80
    throws or breaks things on purpose, 85
    too easily frustrated, 80
    too "grabby," impulsive, 84
    upset by every little thing, 79

"I" messages, 80–82
ICD-9, *see International Classification of Diseases, Ninth Edition*
IEP, *see* Individualized education program
IFSP, *see* Individualized family service plan
Implementing interventions, 67, 69–70
Impulsivity, 3, 11, 14, 15, 18, 19, 84
In vivo systematic desensitization, 76
Inconsolability, 3, 26, 36, 79–80
Indicators of unusual behaviors, 8
Individualized education program (IEP), 4, 4*t*, 25, 33
Individualized family service plan (IFSP), 4, 4*t*, 25, 68
Internal consistency
  of TABS Assessment Tool, 51–52, 52*t*, 53*t*
  of TABS Screener, 57
International Classification of Diseases (ICD-9), 5
Interpreting scores, 45–46, 46*f*–48*f*
  see also Scoring TABS Screener and Assessment Tool
  Need Help indicators, 24–25
  subtest scores of TABS Assessment Tool, 24, 24*f*
  TABS Screener raw score, 23
  Temperament and Regulatory Index, 23–24, 24*f*
Intervention, 1, 4, 63–93
  illustration of intervention program, 67–70
  lead agencies for, 25
  model for community-based, family-centered early intervention, 64–67
    assess behavior, function, and risk/protective factors, 65–66, 68–69
    collect baseline data on problem behavior, 66, 69
    evaluate progress, 67, 70
    identify problem and restate it as goal, 65, 68
    implement intervention and ensure correct implementation, 67, 69–70
    monitor progress and implementation, 67, 70
    plan intervention, 66–67, 69
    specify objective for intervention, 66, 69
  need for early intervention, 63–64
  research-based, 71–93
    for detached items, 72–79
    for dysregulated items, 91–93
    for hyper-sensitive/active items, 79–86
    for underreactive items, 86–91
Irritability, 3, 11, 14–16, 36, 81
Item development, 1, 35–40
  55-item TABS Assessment Tool, 38–40, 38*f*, 39*t*–40*t*
  final steps in item selection, 37–38
  preliminary steps in item selection, 36–37
  selecting items for TABS Screener, 40

Jealousy, 83

Language, 13, 29
Laughter, 72, 86–87
Learned helplessness, 80, 82
Learning disabilities, 13, 16

Means for TABS scores, 23, 52, 53*t*
Mental retardation, 13, 17
Monitoring progress, 67, 70
Mood swings, 80
Motor-sensory processing difficulty, 11, 18, 19
Motorically disorganized behavior, 11, 18, 19

Need Help indicators
  explaining use of, 21, 22
  interpretation of, 24–25
Negative reactivity, 2, 9, 11, 18
Neurobehavioral markers (phenotypes), 8, 12–17
  for acquired brain injury, 17
  for attention-deficit/hyperactivity disorder, 14
  for autism spectrum disorder, 13–14
  for fetal alcohol syndrome and drug exposure, 14–15
  for fragile X syndrome, 13
  for neurofibromatosis, 15–16
  for regulatory disorders, 12–13
  for Rett syndrome, 16–17
  for seizure disorder, 15
  for Sotos syndrome, 17
  for Williams syndrome, 16
Neurobehavioral organization, 9–10
Neurofibromatosis, 15–16
Neurological impairment, 3, 8, 12
Noncompliance, 3, 10, 14, 18, 71, 84–85
Norms for TABS, 40–44
  agencies and organizations contributing to TABS sample, 99–104
  characteristics of normative sample, 41, 42*t*
  characteristics of sample of children with disabilities, 42–44, 44*t*, 45*t*
  sampling procedures, 40–41
  selecting normative sample of children without disabilities, 41
  TABS performance of normative sample, 42, 42*t*, 43*t*
Novelty reactivity, 9

Oppositional-defiant disorder, 10
  see also Defiant behavior
Overreactive style of behavior, 3, 11, 18

Parent–Child Interaction Therapy (PCIT), 84–85
Parents
  completion of TABS Screener and Assessment Tool by, 4–5, 21–22
  explaining TABS to, 21–22
  risk/protective factors for problem behaviors related to, 66
PCIT, *see* Parent–Child Interaction Therapy
PDD, *see* Pervasive developmental disorder
Percentiles, 44, 59, 105*t*
Pervasive developmental disorder (PDD), 10, 30, 87–90
Piaget, Jean, 5
Planning interventions, 66–67, 69
Play, 73, 75, 88–89
Positive affectivity, 9
Prenatal drug exposure, 10, 14–15, 36
Preschool Language Scale, 30
Prosthetic devices, 12
Purposes of TABS, 3–4, 4*t*

Reading level of TABS, 5
Regulatory disorders, 12–13
  definition of, 13, 18
  diagnostic classification of, 10–11
    TABS normative research as empirical validation of, 17–19, 19*t*
  neurobehavioral organization and, 9–10
  types of, 10–11, 18–19
  see also Temperament and self-regulation
Relationship risk/protective factors, 66
Reliability of TABS scores, 51–52, 52*t*, 53*t*
Reluctant speech, 90
Research applications of TABS, 4, 4*t*
Research foundations of TABS, 7–20
Research-based specific interventions, 71–93
  for detached items, 72–79
  for dysregulated items, 91–93
  for hyper-sensitive/active items, 79–86
  for underreactive items, 86–91
Rett syndrome, 16–17
Risk/protective factors for problem behaviors, 65–66, 68–69

Sampling procedures, 40–41
  see also Norms for TABS
Schedule changes and transitions, 15, 72
Score cutoffs for program eligibility and wraparound mental health behavioral support, 25, 46, 49
Scoring TABS Screener and Assessment Tool, 5–6, 22–25
  see also Interpreting scores
  completing TABS Assessment Tool summary, 23
  computing TABS Screener raw score, 22–23
  consistency of scores, 51–52, 52*t*, 53*t*
  derived scores, 44, 45*t*, 105*t*
    accuracy of, 59–60
  scores for children with and without disabilities, 58
  scores related to age and sex, 58
  stability of scores, 54–57, 55*t*–57*t*

standard errors of measurement for scores, 53, 54*t*
validity of scores, 57–61, 59*f*, 60*f*, 60*t*
Screening, *see* TABS Screener
Seizure disorders, 12, 15, 74–75
Self-absorption, 3, 18
Self-control strategies, 80
Self-regulation, *see* Temperament and self-regulation
Shyness, 11
Situational transitions, 15, 72
Sleep disturbances, 1, 3, 11, 13, 15, 26, 36, 91–93
"Slow-to-warm" style of behavior, 11
Social deficits, 15, 16
Social-skills training, 80
Sotos syndrome, 17
Split half reliability correlations for TABS scores, 51–52, 52*t*
Stability of TABS scores, 54–57, 55*t*
internal consistency of TABS Screener, 57
reliability of differences between subtest scores, 55–57, 56*t*, 57*t*
Standard deviations for TABS scores, 23, 52, 53*t*
Standard errors of measurement for TABS scores, 53, 54*t*
Standard scores, 44, 59, 105*t*
Standard scores normalized by area transformation, 44, 105*t*
Stereotypic movements, 16, 78
Subtests of TABS Assessment Tool
derived scores for, 105*t*
interpreting scores on, 24, 24*f*
reliability of differences between subtest scores, 55–57, 56*t*, 57*t*
reliability of scores on, 51–52, 52*t*, 53*t*
standard errors of measurement for scores on, 53, 54*t*
Factor 1: Detached, 3
Factor 2: Hyper-sensitive/active, 3
Factor 3: Underreactive, 3
Factor 4: Dysregulated, 3
vignettes illustrating use of, 26–29, 31–33
Systematic desensitization, 76

TABS, *see* Temperament and Atypical Behavior Scale
TABS Assessment Tool, 2
administration of, 4–5, 21–22
completing Section I on first page of, 22
scoring and interpretation of, 5–6, 23–25, 44–46, 46*f*–48*f*
categorization of scores, 59–60
completing summary, 23
consistency of scores, 51–52, 52*t*, 53*t*
derived scores, 44, 45*t*, 105*t*
interpreting *Need Help* indicators, 24–25
interpreting subtest scores, 24, 24*f*
interpreting Temperament and Regulatory Index, 23–24, 24*f*
stability of scores, 54–57, 55*t*–57*t*
selecting items for, 35–40
target behaviors for, 5
time required for completion of, 22
vignettes illustrating use of, 26–33, 26*f*–33*f*, 28*t*, 29*t*, 32*t*
TABS Screener, 2
administration of, 4–5, 21–22
completing identifying data on, 22
cutoff scores for, 25, 46, 49
internal consistency of, 57
number of items on, 40
scoring and interpretation of, 5–6
computing raw score, 22–23
interpreting raw score, 23
selecting items for, 40
time required for completion of, 22
validity of, 40, 60–61
vignette illustrating use of, 30, 30*f*
Technical adequacy of TABS, 51–61
consistency of TABS scores, 51–52
internal consistency, 51–52, 52*t*, 53*t*
stability of scores, 54–57, 55*t*
internal consistency of TABS Screener, 57
reliability of differences between subtest scores, 55–57, 56*t*, 57*t*
standard errors of measurement, 53, 54*t*
validity, 57–61
categorization of scores, 59–60
construct validity, 58–59, 60*f*, 61*f*, 61*t*
content validity, 57–58
of TABS Screener, 60–61
Temper tantrums, 6, 11, 12, 14, 16, 26, 29, 81
Temperament and Atypical Behavior Scale (TABS), 1–6
administration of, 4–5, 21–22
agencies and organizations contributing to TABS sample, 101–106
ages assessed by, 1
areas assessed by, 2
completion by parents, 4–5, 21–22
components of, 3
content summary of, 2–3
development of, 1, 35–49
number of items on, 2, 21
purposes of, 3–4, 4*t*
reading level of, 5
research applications of, 4
research foundations of, 7–20
scoring and interpretation of, 5–6, 22–25
subtests of, 3

Temperament and Atypical Behavior Scale (TABS)—*continued*
technical adequacy of, 51–61
time required for completion of, 22
used as part of comprehensive assessment battery, 4
vignettes illustrating use of, 26–33
Temperament and Regulatory Index (TRI), 23–24, 40
categorization of scores on, 59–60
derived scores for, 105*t*
prediction from TABS Screener score, 46, 49
reliability of, 51–52, 52*t*, 53*t*
stability coefficient for, 54
Temperament and self-regulation, 7–20
atypical development, 8–9
atypical self-regulation and neurobehavioral organization, 9–10
conceptual and research schemes for disorders of, 9
core attributes of typical development, 9
definitions related to, 7–9
diagnostic classification of regulatory disorders, 10–11
TABS normative research as empirical validation of, 17–19, 19*t*
extremes in temperamental styles, 11–12
indicators of unusual behaviors, 8
mismatch between child's temperament and caregivers' responses, 12
neurobehavioral markers for unusual behaviors, 8, 12–17
typical developmental progression for self-regulation, 9
Time-out, 81
Timidity, 11
Tourette syndrome, 75
Toys, 75, 77, 89–90
Transitions, 15, 72
TRI, *see* Temperament and Regulatory Index
"Tuning out," 74–75

Underreactive style of temperament, 3, 10, 16, 18–19
derived scores for, 105*t*
interventions for, 86–91
almost never babbles or tries to talk, 90
doesn't care when others are hurt, 88
doesn't enjoy playing with mother or caregiver, 89
doesn't pay attention to sights and sounds, 87
doesn't play much at all, 88–89
doesn't react to own name, 88
doesn't react to sounds, 90
doesn't seem to watch moving objects, 87
is not upset when toy is taken away, 89–90
rarely smiles, giggles, or laughs at funny things, 86–87
shows no surprise to new events, 87–88

Validity of TABS scores, 57–61
categorization of scores, 59–60
construct validity, 58–59, 60*f*, 61*f*, 61*t*
content validity, 57–58
definition of, 57
TABS Screener, 40, 60–61
Vignettes illustrating use of TABS Assessment Tool, 26–33, 26*f*–33*f*, 28*t*, 29*t*, 32*t*

Wandering, 78–79
Williams syndrome, 5, 16
Wraparound mental health behavioral support, 4, 25
TABS cutoff scores and eligibility for, 25, 46, 49